T0291397

Enhancing Intercultural Communication in Organizations

This book provides a qualitative analysis of the process of consultancy, to prove how intercultural communication can solve issues rising from multiculturalism in organizations and policymaking.

Experts in intercultural consultancy examine 12 different cases from real situations, focusing on interviews with clients and the way advice is presented and discussed with them, and on collected data and the process by which it is gathered. The book proves how the mechanisms of intercultural communication can be used to foster respectful relationships between people of different cultural and linguistic backgrounds and contribute to the success of the project or organization in question.

This book will be a key resource for scholars and students involved in intercultural communication, management, and consultancy, as well as professionals that are confronted in their work with diversity and would like to know more about intercultural consultancy.

Additional questions for discussion and readings are available as e-resources on the Routledge website.

Roos Beerkens works as a lecturer at the Department of Language, Literature and Communication, University of Utrecht. She teaches within the Master's programme in Intercultural Communication and is the internship coordinator for the programme. She has gained experience as a trainer in intercultural competences and is working on research concerning the effectiveness of intercultural competences training. She received a summa cum laude for her PhD research at the University of Münster, Germany, where she analysed Dutch-German communication in the border area. She has five years of experience as a communication consultant in the field of internal intercultural communication. She worked for a communication agency, carrying out projects for a variety of organizations.

Emmanuelle Le Pichon-Vorstman is a lecturer at Utrecht University and at the University of Toronto, Ontario Institute for Studies in Education. She is Head of the Centre de Recherches en Éducation Franco-Ontarienne (CRÉFO). Her keen interest in migration policy has led her to conduct research studies on issues related to multilingual education, particularly on the education of newly arrived migrant pupils in Europe and indigenous pupils in Suriname in collaboration with the Rutu Foundation. She has worked as a consultant, researcher, evaluator, and reviewer for several international organizations and international journals. She has participated in policy analyses, notably for the European Commission and the Migration Policy Institute.

Roselinde Supheert received her MPhil degree in linguistics from Cambridge University (1985) and obtained her PhD degree at Utrecht University (1995). Her research focuses on reception and intercultural communication. She teaches English language and literature, and intercultural communication, at Utrecht University. She has also worked as adviser to the English Department and to the Faculty of Humanities of Utrecht University in projects including the application of student peer review in proficiency teaching, curriculum development, and English proficiency, and internationalization and the use of non-native English as a classroom language.

Jan D. ten Thije is Professor of Intercultural Communication at the Department of Languages, Literature and Communication at Utrecht University. His main fields of research concern institutional discourse in multicultural and international settings, receptive multilingualism, intercultural training, language education, and functional pragmatics. Since 2007 he has coordinated the Master's programme in Intercultural Communication. He is connected to the Utrecht Institute of Linguistics (UiL-OTS) at the Department of Languages, Literature and Communication at Utrecht University. He has been engaged in intercultural counselling and training activities in urban, academic, and European Committee constellations.

Routledge Focus on Communication Studies

A Relational Model of Public Discourse
The African Philosophy of Ubuntu
Leyla Tavernaro-Haidarian

Communicating Science and Technology through Online Video
Researching a New Media Phenomenon
Edited by Bienvenido León and Michael Bourk

Strategic Communication and Deformative Transparency
Persuasion in Politics, Propaganda, and Public Health
Isaac Nahon-Serfaty

Globalism and Gendering Cancer
Tracking the Trope of Oncogenic Women from the US to Kenya
Miriam O'Kane Mara

Maatian Ethics in a Communication Context
Melba Vélez Ortiz

Enhancing Intercultural Communication in Organizations
Insights From Project Advisers
Edited by Roos Beerkens, Emmanuelle Le Pichon-Vorstman, Roselinde Supheert, and Jan D. ten Thije

Enhancing Intercultural Communication in Organizations

Insights From Project Advisers

**Edited by
Roos Beerkens,
Emmanuelle Le Pichon-Vorstman,
Roselinde Supheert, and
Jan D. ten Thije**

Routledge
Taylor & Francis Group

NEW YORK AND LONDON

First published 2020
by Routledge
52 Vanderbilt Avenue, New York, NY 10017

and by Routledge
2 Park Square, Milton Park, Abingdon, Oxon, OX14 4RN

Routledge is an imprint of the Taylor & Francis Group, an informa business

Library of Congress Cataloging-in-Publication Data
A catalog record for this book has been requested

ISBN: 978-0-367-43963-7 (hbk)
ISBN: 978-1-003-00679-4 (ebk)

Typeset in Times New Roman
by Apex Covantage.LLC

Visit eResources at: www.routledge.com/9780367439637

Contents

List of Figures and Images   x
List of Tables   xi
List of Contributors   xii
Foreword   xvii
MARIE-CHRISTINE KOK ESCALLE

1   Introduction   1
ROOS BEERKENS, EMMANUELLE LE PICHON-VORSTMAN,
ROSELINDE SUPHEERT, AND JAN D. TEN THIJE

2   Key Concepts   5
ROOS BEERKENS AND EMMANUELLE LE PICHON-VORSTMAN

PART I
Policymakers   13

**Case Study 1 Advising Municipalities on Schooling Newly
     Arrived Migrant Pupils**   15
EMMANUELLE LE PICHON-VORSTMAN AND SERGIO BAAUW

**Case Study 2 Intercultural Communication Between a
     Municipality and Polish Migrants**   22
DARIA VAN KOLCK (BORUTA) AND PAULINA WOŁOSZYN

**Case Study 3 Internal Communication at the
     University of Aruba**   34
ERIC MIJTS, ROSELINDE SUPHEERT, AND FARDAU BAMBERGER

**Case Study 4 Lingua Receptiva at the Directorate-General
for Translation (DGT) of the European Commission**   45
JAN D. TEN THIJE

**PART II
Commercial Organizations**   55

**Case Study 5 Acquisition Within One Country: How Two
Organizational Cultures Come Together**   57
ROOS BEERKENS

**Case Study 6 Enhancing Team Effectiveness for an
Executive Team in Saudi Arabia**   66
JÜRGEN HELL, JULES BOLHUIS, AND ROSELINDE SUPHEERT

**PART III
Education**   75

**Case Study 7 Advising Parents on Bilingual Education of
Their Children**   77
MANUELA PINTO

**Case Study 8 Advising Linguistically Diverse Schools on
Developing a School-wide Language Policy**   83
KOEN VAN GORP AND PANDORA VERSTEDEN

**Case Study 9 Shifting From a Monolingual to a Plurilingual
Pedagogical Practice**   93
MARIE-PAULE LORY

**PART IV
Non-Profit Organizations**   103

**Case Study 10 Improving Specialized Mental Healthcare
and Social Services for Deaf and Hard of Hearing
Newcomers**   105
ANNE BERGHUIS

Case Study 11 A Model Village Constitution for Indigenous Traditional Leaders in Suriname 113

ELLEN-ROSE KAMBEL AND CAROLINE DE JONG

Case Study 12 Photographers' Handling of Cultural Rituals and Conventions of Bereaved Parents After the Loss of a Child 124

MAAIKE AANS AND WIEKE EEFTING

Concluding Chapter 134

ROOS BEERKENS AND EMMANUELLE LE PICHON-VORSTMAN

Subject Index 138
Name Index 142

Figures and Images

2.1 A Poster in Polish (English: Are you looking for a good book? Now you can borrow Polish books at BiblioNu) at the Entrance of the Library [30 April 2015] 25

2.2 Dutch and Polish Texts (English: Almost for free) Observed at the Jumble Sale [3 May 2015] 26

2.3 The Information Board in the Centre of Horst With the Poster Inside [25 April 2015] 27

3.1 Organization Chart of the UA 35

5.1 The Zipper Metaphor Used to Illustrate the Integration Process 61

6.1 Organization Chart of the Company 67

8.1 Three Circles of a Powerful Learning Environment 86

11.1 Village Leaders Discussing the Outcome of the Village Consultations (2007) 118

12.1 Praxeogram Process of Photoshoots 126

Tables

3.1	Overview of Observed Meetings	37
3.2	List of Participants	38
6.1	Timeline for Research and Intervention	68

Contributors

Maaike Aans completed her Master's degree in Intercultural Communication (*Cum Laude*) at Utrecht University, the Netherlands, in 2017. Since then, she has worked as an intercultural trainer and consultant. She is currently working as Training and Research Fellow for Clingendael, the Netherlands Institute of International Relations. She trains and advises diplomats and international professionals from all over the world by supporting them in becoming effective communicators across cultural borders. In her work, Maaike has travelled to a range of countries, including Ethiopia, Algeria, Germany, Belgium and Georgia to give lectures and trainings on Intercultural Communication.

Sergio Baauw is Assistant Professor at the Spanish Language and Culture Programme of Utrecht University, and is also active in the Master's programmes in Intercultural Communication and Multilingualism and Language Acquisition. His research focuses on first and second language acquisition, multilingualism, and language impairment. He has been involved in consultancy work on education for newly arrived migrant pupils, together with Emmanuelle Le Pichon-Vorstman. This research was focused on measuring the academic development of newly arrived migrant pupils during their stay at a special reception school, and after their transition to the regular Dutch primary schools. The advice was submitted to the Municipality of Utrecht in August 2015.

Fardau Bamberger studied English Language and Culture in Groningen and Intercultural Communication at the University of Utrecht. She worked as a communications intern at the University of Aruba, where she also took part in the UAUCU research project and wrote her Master's thesis on the role of English in Aruba's linguistic landscape. She graduated in 2016 and is now working at the Communications Office of the University of Groningen as a news editor.

Roos Beerkens works as a lecturer at the Department of Language, Literature and Communication, University of Utrecht. She teaches within the

Master's programme in Intercultural Communication and is the internship coordinator for the programme. She has gained experience as a trainer in intercultural competences and is working on research concerning the effectiveness of intercultural competences training. She received a summa cum laude for her PhD research at the University of Münster, Germany, where she analysed Dutch-German communication in the border area. She has five years of experience as a communication consultant in the field of internal intercultural communication. She worked for a communication agency, carrying out projects for a variety of organizations.

Anne Berghuis was born and raised in Voorburg, the Netherlands. She received a BA in English Language and Culture from Utrecht University in 2015 and an MA in Intercultural Communication from Utrecht University in 2016. While studying for her MA, she joined the international Eurocampus programme, which was held in Cambridge, United Kingdom, and afterwards wrote her thesis on language attitude among the indigenous people of Suriname in regard to the dimensions, language choice, language dominance, and language preference. She completed her Master's year with an internship at a mental health and social services organization for the deaf and hard of hearing, where she conducted research on ways to improve the support system for deaf and hard of hearing refugees in the Netherlands from the perspective of intercultural communication dimensions.

Jules Bolhuis stayed in Saudi Arabia as a management consultant intern for Nahdi Medical Company in 2016. In 2013, he lived in Cairo for seven months to study Arabic. He has great affinity with the Middle East and North Africa region. More recently, he graduated from the University of Utrecht Master's programme in Intercultural Communication and specialized in intercultural competencies.

Daria van Kolck (Boruta) was born and raised in Poland, where she obtained her Bachelor's degree in Dutch Studies at Adam Mickiewicz University in Poznan. In 2015 she graduated from Utrecht University, the Netherlands, with a Master's degree in Intercultural Communication. She has been working in the communication sector.

Wieke Eefting holds a PhD in Linguistics and currently has a management position at Utrecht University. In addition, as a freelance photographer, she is involved in the work of the Foundation Make a Memory. She works for the Foundation on a voluntary basis and produces photo series for bereaved parents with different cultural, religious and ethnic backgrounds. She is also a member of the executive board of the Foundation *Taal Doet Meer*, an NGO providing language acquisition programs for inhabitants of Utrecht with a non-Western background. With her background in research and photography in a multicultural setting, she acted as a liaison between the Foundation and the principal researcher of the present study.

Koen Van Gorp is Head of Foreign Language Assessment at the Center for Language Teaching Advancement, and Affiliated Faculty in the MA TESOL and Second Language Studies PhD Program at Michigan State University. He also serves as a research fellow at the Centre for Language and Education, KU Leuven, Belgium.

Jürgen Hell is MSc in Organizational Psychology and in Clinical Psychology. He is Team Facilitator and Leadership Coach at Teamcoaching.one, and teaches occupational and organizational psychology at Radboud University, Nijmegen, the Netherlands. With 25 years of experience as a consultant, he specialized in leadership and team development and works for a variety of mainly international clients. He has a particular interest for the impact of cultural differences and psychological diversity on organizational effectiveness.

Caroline de Jong holds an MA degree in Non-western History (University of Groningen, the Netherlands) and has over 12 years of experience working on indigenous peoples' issues, including research and trainings for and with communities. Between 2004 and 2006 she worked as an independent consultant, and since 2006 she has been working with the Forest Peoples Programme, an NGO based in the United Kingdom that supports the rights of indigenous peoples.

Ellen-Rose Kambel obtained a law degree and a PhD in Social Sciences from the University of Leiden. She has worked for over 15 years as a human rights trainer and consultant with indigenous peoples and for international organizations including the Inter-American Development Bank, UNICEF, ILO, and the Rainforest Foundation. She is the co-founder and currently director of the Rutu Foundation for Intercultural Multilingual Education, which is dedicated to achieving quality education for indigenous and ethnic minority children around the world. She is the author of several publications on the rights of indigenous peoples, indigenous women, and the education of indigenous and migrant children.

Marie-Christine Kok Escalle studied History at Université Paris Sorbonne and Semiotics at the EPHE (Paris). She obtained her PhD at Utrecht University, where she worked as Associate Professor, teaching French culture, and initiated and developed the Utrecht MA Programme in Intercultural Communication. After her retirement she continued as Senior Researcher at the Institute for Cultural Inquiry (Utrecht University). Her scholarly interests include the cultural role French language and culture has played in the Netherlands, focusing, for the last 20 years, on the development of intercultural competence through foreign language learning and teaching, in the past as well as nowadays.

Eric Mijts studied Linguistics and Literature at the University of Antwerp and is specialized in sociolinguistics. In 2000 he joined the University of Aruba, where he works as a researcher and lecturer in skills and linguistics. He coordinates the Academic Foundation Year and the UAUCU undergraduate research exchange program. His research and publications focus on multilingualism, language policy and planning, identity, and social inclusion/exclusion processes.

Emmanuelle Le Pichon-Vorstman is a lecturer at Utrecht University and at the University of Toronto, Ontario Institute for Studies in Education. She is Head of the Centre de Recherches en Éducation Franco-Ontarienne (CRÉFO). Her keen interest in migration policy has led her to conduct research studies on issues related to multilingual education, particularly on the education of newly arrived migrant pupils in Europe and indigenous pupils in Suriname in collaboration with the Rutu Foundation. She has worked as a consultant, researcher, evaluator, and reviewer for several international organizations and international journals. She has participated in policy analyses, notably for the European Commission and the Migration Policy Institute.

Marie-Paule Lory holds a PhD in Didactics and she is an assistant professor at the University of Toronto. Her main areas of interest are linguistic representations among language learners and the inclusion of linguistic and cultural diversity in teaching practices. She is also the president of the international association EDILIC (Education et diversité linguistique et culturelle).

Manuela Pinto is Assistant Professor of Italian Language and Linguistics at the Department of Modern Languages at Utrecht University. She has a solid theoretical background in generative grammar, but her research interests go far beyond syntax and include semantics, discourse-pragmatics, and language development. Her current research interests focus on grammatical development in L1 and 2L1, particularly with respect to the acquisition of reference and of discourse-tracking devices. She is also committed to making scientific knowledge accessible to common people: together with colleagues Sharon Unsworth and Ivana Brasileiro she offers workshops about raising children bilingually, and she is creating a virtual information service for bilingual families and other people interested in raising children bilingually.

Rosanne Severs holds a Master's degree in Intercultural Communication from Utrecht University. She is Director of Globi, Utrecht, a company that focuses on internationalization and intercultural learning, aiming to stimulate the development of intercultural and educational skills by developing educational materials, trainings, study visits, and exchange programmes between Dutch, Chinese, and Indian educational institutions.

Roselinde Supheert received her MPhil degree in Linguistics from Cambridge University (1985) and obtained her PhD degree at Utrecht University (1995). Her research focuses on reception and intercultural communication. She teaches English language and literature, and intercultural communication at Utrecht University. She has also worked as adviser to the English Department and to the Faculty of Humanities of Utrecht University in projects including the application of student peer review in proficiency teaching, curriculum development, and English proficiency, and internationalization and the use of non-native English as a classroom language.

Jan D. ten Thije is Professor of Intercultural Communication at the Department of Languages, Literature and Communication at Utrecht University. His main fields of research concern institutional discourse in multicultural and international settings, receptive multilingualism, intercultural training, language education, and functional pragmatics. Since 2007 he has coordinated the Master's programme in Intercultural Communication. He is connected to the Utrecht Institute of Linguistics (UiL-OTS) at the Department of Languages, Literature and Communication at Utrecht University. He has been engaged in intercultural counselling and training activities in urban, academic, and European Committee constellations.

Pandora Versteden coordinates the trainers section of the Centre for Language and Education (CLE), KU Leuven (Belgium). Since 2012 she has been a language policy consultant for the CLE in different areas in Flanders, including Genk.

Paulina Wołoszyn grew up in Wroclaw, Poland. She obtained her Bachelor's degree in Dutch Philology at Wroclaw University. She also studied Dutch at the University of Vienna. In 2016 she moved to the Netherlands where, in 2017, she graduated from Utrecht University with a Master's degree in Intercultural Communication. After her studies Paulina worked in the financial sector in the Netherlands. She has recently moved to Poland.

Foreword
Theory – Practice

Marie-Christine Kok Escalle

For millennia, philosophers have been interrogating the relation between theory and practice. Already at the Greek Academy, Plato's *Gorgias*, for example (521d), describes how Socrates examines to what extent Athenians link pragmatic action to theory. Plato represents Socrates describing the importance of political involvement while saying, "I think that I am the only or almost the only Athenian living who practises the true art of politics; I am the only politician of my time."[1]

Universities today echo his dialogue stressing the importance of the relationship between theory and daily practice. This relationship is particularly relevant in modern language programmes with a focus on intercultural communication. Clearly, a book on intercultural consultancy has a place in academic programmes offering instruction in intercultural relations. However, to understand the reality of an intercultural space, the concept must be viewed in the wider context of *Agreeing to Disagree* (*La mésentente cordiale*), as posited by Geoffroy.[2] The choice for academic consultancy in intercultural communication is as interesting as the process of consultancy. The present publication considers both.

In the 1980s a call to action with respect to research in the field of (inter)cultural communication was answered by the Department of French Language and Culture at Utrecht University when their teachers/researchers, reflecting on current contexts and teaching practices and on the need for changes due to newly defined global circumstances, redesigned their teaching related to intercultural communication pairing academic disciplines with consultancy in a twin relationship.

Universities in Quebec in the 1970s had begun to shape intercultural theory through the discussion of intercultural communication and the topic was taken up in Europe in the 1980s and 1990s. Particularly influential in this was the worldwide network of French culture teachers (*culture* replacing the usual term *civilisation*), also influenced by postmodern and postcolonial thought, who situated their approach of culture in relation to interculturality. At Utrecht University, the teaching of French culture (*culture française*) had traditionally included the sociology of Bourdieu[3] and the semiotics of Greimas. In the 1990s instruction expanded to include an intercultural dimension through multiple analyses of French society, and students were given tools that they could later apply in professional contexts. Their teachers were aware of the many facets of intercultural studies, such as developments in student motivations for studying modern languages, the variety of social science disciplines available, and changing socio-economic realities, and as a result designed programmes using innovative approaches to learning. Economic globalization increased and students working in a professional space required plurilingual and pluricultural[4] competences that included intercultural communicative competences for use in international exchanges. The development of new approaches to teaching modern languages and culture led to the sharing of pedagogical views of the departments of French and German.[5] They agreed that all future teaching was to include an intercultural dimension.

Another impetus behind transformations within the university curriculum was that students of law, administration, politics, or business were becoming aware that intercultural competency was vital to their future. The development of new programmes, especially in modern languages, where instruction now included pragmatic use of language and applied skills in foreign socio-cultural practices, catered to their needs. Utrecht students of French language and culture noticed and asked for an essential expansion of a theoretical base in the direction of applied cultural practice, choosing public relations, mass media, international business, or commercial finance as free options in their curricula; in this, they added a valuable component for their future professional life to their plurilingual competency. Their awareness was stimulated by the perspective of cultural anthropology and interactional sociology in their courses about culture and identity, and culture and communication in a historical context.

Observing the need and aspiration for plurilingual competency in my students and encouraged by Professor Maarten van Buuren in the Department of French Literature, I developed and led a graduate programme[6] on French language and culture designed specifically for students wanting to work in international business/management or international organizations (including diplomacy). Students who enrolled in this programme prepared for international careers and developed not only linguistic and cultural competencies but also learned to identify and analyse relevant parameters at work in systems functioning in the context of a modern language and culture. The programme at Utrecht University was unique in that it was intended for students of French language and culture,[7] offering a programme which included two internships, one short and one long, increasing the curriculum from four to five years to allow students to alternate classroom and work floor;[8] studying *en alternance*, to use the French expression, they learned theory in the class-room and gained first-hand experience working in the field. The goal was to ensure that students developed a solid understanding of social and cultural forces, including historical contexts in French or francophone economics, as well as the social interrelations within workplaces where communication occurs in French. Such students are well prepared for a career in a French or francophone company and confident of their ability to give advice if neces-sary, to facilitate intercultural communication, identify problems, and offer effective solutions.

This graduate French language and culture programme was successful for five years (1999–2004), until the reform of Dutch universities introduced the distinction between BA and MA. It was an obvious model, inspiring French and German colleagues at Utrecht University, who found the French programme absolutely relevant, to propose a Master's programme in Inter-cultural Communication, representative of innovative reforms within univer-sities in the Netherlands. The Master's programme started in 2004.[9] It offers a synthesis of theoretical knowledge and practice, teaching students to act responsibly using competencies appropriate to intercultural understanding. It includes instruction in consultancy, using academic reasoning, compara-tive studies, analysis and synthesis, and is intended to develop proactive skills in identifying problems and proposing solutions. The Master's degree in Intercultural Communication has proved to be as attractive as the French programme *en alternance*, which also offered obligatory internships. The Master's degree answers the needs of future professionals who will be work-ing in mediation and remediation in diverse environments. This book was first written for them.

Several of the Master's theses written in partial fulfillment of the require-ments of this programme reflect students' analyses of problematic commu-nication in situations typically found in companies or organizations. The students work within a linguistic and cultural framework of their choice and demonstrate the ability to analyse various documents and interpret formal inquiries that may occur in multilingual and multicultural constellations, including recognizing cultural connotations and their effects on the function-ing of all kinds of organizational systems. This programme offers solutions to appreciate the complexities of *otherness*.

University staff, experienced in educating students in professional media-tion in intercultural contexts, may well function as advisers on policy matters, on programmatic and operational, or on economic issues, such as business administration. Academic researchers and teachers can be agents for social cohesion: trainers in mediation in multilingual and multicultural contexts. As intercultural mediators with intercultural experience, they are able to interpret complexities in multilingual and multicultural communication in terms of the plurality of identities and to adopt "strategies of explanation, negotiation or mediation"[10] as required. This qualitative approach, analysing the processes in consultancy and reflecting on the practices, is found in the different case studies presented in this book, which illustrates various activities of a researcher at work as an academic and a socially embedded agent.

The initiatives at the Dutch university which in Utrecht led to the Master's programme in Intercultural Communication were also inspired by research activities led by Geneviève Zarate (INALCO, Paris) and her colleagues, at the European Council of the European Centre for Modern Languages (Graz, Austria) from 2000 till 2004, examining "the social role of the cultural mediator in a plurilingual situation," a role exemplified by the modern language teacher, and well suited to the goal of the European Council of the European Centre for Modern Languages, to promote education in the field of mediation as a part of European development. In addition, the work of John Gumperz and his colleagues on Discourse Strategies in interethnic communication (1982) and Michael Agar on Language Shock (1994) is addressed in the Master's programme at Utrecht University.[11]

Over the past few decades, Philippe d'Iribarne and his team at the Laboratory CNRS "Management and Society" have conducted research complementary to the previously mentioned multilingual and multicultural instruction. Looking at multilingualism and multiculturalism from an economic or political angle, their approach differs from that of language teachers, and their work sheds a cultural light on, for instance, business management studies, showing that a commercial organization is itself a mirror of society. D'Iribarne "has identified tools used in understanding pluriculturalism" that can solve problems associated with intercultural management on the micro/macro scale in (inter)national companies and has developed possible political solutions to social problems arising from human migration and commercial displacement.[12] In the Utrecht Master's programme, this initial focus has been broadened to the analysis of linguistic and cultural diversity in different kinds of organizational and management constellations.

Commercial and political leaders have a decisive impact on society and may influence intercultural consultation. It is vitally important that the professional people with intercultural expertise who work at universities remain aware of the ethical context to their research and, in the case of consultation, specifically of Bourdieu's concept of *habitus*. Being aware of the position and the role of the consultant, as mentioned in the introduction to this book, is of ethical importance. It appears clearly in the analyses of the case studies in different fields and settings, namely *counselling policymakers, commercial consultancy, consultancy in education, and counselling non-profit organizations.*

Notes

1. Paul Demont, "Socrate et l'ἀπραγμοσύνη (apragmosynè) chez Plato", Études platoniciennes [http://journals.openedition.org/etudesplatoniciennes/763].
2. Christine Geoffroy, *La mésentente cordiale, Voyage au cœur de l'espace interculturel franco-anglais*, Grasset 2001.
3. In the 1990s, several of the author's seminars concerned the works of Pierre Bourdieu, whom the students had the occasion to meet when he visited Amsterdam. Bourdieu is the first of the professors at the *Collège de France* to have lectured outside its walls.
4. In Europe *plurilingualism* applies to individuals and *multilingualism* applies to societies, whereas in the Anglo-American literature multilingualism (and multiculturalism) are both individual and societal phenomena.
5. Notably of the author, who held the position of Senior Lecturer in French Culture, and Professor Dr. Wolfgang Herrlitz, Professor in Educational Linguistics and German Language.
6. This ambitious programme could be chosen by students from their third year onwards and included general and French courses, combining a general introduction to international communication, to governance and management, and economy with language-specific courses like French for lawyers, economists, businesses, and French sociolinguistics and cultural issues such as connotations in French communication systems, cultural politics and identities, and human resources and economic systems in France.
7. A programme on "international business communication" [*internationale bedrijfscommunicatie*] existed at the University of Nijmegen offering a language and cultural component (French or Spanish) for students in international business studies.
8. Thanks to Prof. Dr. Maarten van Buuren from the French Department, the dual programme received funding from the Minister of Education for two years (viz. 1999–2001). Unfortunately, the German Department, which had also submitted a request for funding, was rejected and therefore was unable to offer a programme similar to the French at the start of the Ba-Ma system.
9. Herrlitz and Kok Escalle were rapidly joined by Jan ten Thije from the Department of Dutch Language and Culture. The Master's programme in Intercultural Communication has, from the beginning, included all modern languages: Dutch, English, French, German, Italian, (Portuguese) and Spanish languages and cultures.
10. Geneviève Zarate (INALCO, Paris), Aline Gohard-Radenkovic (Fribourg, Switz.), Denise Lussier (McGill University, Canada), and Hermine Penz (Graz, Austria), *Cultural Mediation in Language Learning and Teaching*, European Centre for Modern Languages Council of Europe 2004, 230–231. This book is the product of research activities at the European Centre for Modern Languages in Graz (Austria) during four years (2000–2004); Kok Escalle has been taking part in this international research group.

11. John J. Gumperz (1982), *Discourse Strategies*. Cambridge: Cambridge University Press; Michael Agar (1996), *Language Shock: Understanding the Culture of Conversation*. New York: HarperCollins.
12. Philippe d'Iribarne, *La logique de l'honneur: Gestion des entreprises et traditions nationales*. Paris: Seuil, 1989; *Cultures et mondialisation: Gérer par delà les frontières*. Paris: Seuil, 1998; *Managing Corporate Values in Diverse National Cultures: The Challenge of Differences*. London: Routledge, 2012; *Les immigrés de la République: les impasses du multiculturalisme*. Paris: Seuil, 2010.

1 Introduction

Roos Beerkens, Emmanuelle Le Pichon-Vorstman,
Roselinde Supheert, and Jan D. ten Thije

The increasing mobility of people implies that interactions between individuals of different cultural backgrounds are commonplace at all levels of
society. In the context of globalization and internationalization, multicultural
groups have become the rule, rather than the exception. In their slipstream
intercultural communication has become an important element in many
fields of academic study, of which intercultural consultancy is among the
most socially relevant, gaining attention over the past years. In our view,
intercultural consultancy is concerned with analysis and advice with respect
to intercultural encounters from a situated view on culture. This means that
research and interventions that aim to facilitate intercultural practices need
to take into account the social, cultural, historical and economic contexts to
which the participants in the exchange belong. In other words, in our view
there is a need to analyse each case on a micro level. This view on culture
and intercultural communication is increasingly supported by academic literature; multicultural teams are in essence fruitful in most settings, as long as
the members know how to get the most out of their diversity. In this book, we
look at the way in which experts in intercultural communication can contribute concretely to intercultural understanding within the confines of an organization. Most agencies that offer intercultural consultancy as a paid service are
reluctant to share their experiences. Perhaps they wish to maintain a certain
illusion that they possess the magic formulas to solve the issues related to "a
problem in intercultural communication."

What This Book Has to Offer

In this book, the authors share the experience they have acquired in the
domain of intercultural consultancy over the past 20 years. They discuss a
number of illustrative cases and use these real-life examples to show that
it is a misrepresentation to designate multiculturality as a problem. The
reader will discover that in reality multiculturality, when approached through

intercultural communication, is not a problem but a solution. This book is not a collection of recipes for intercultural consultancy. The authors believe that there are millions of individuals dealing with millions of different situations involving intercultural communication, each of which is also highly dynamic. The danger of an "intercultural cookbook" would be to adopt an essentialist approach, which would reduce people to cultural affiliation. The approach of this book is qualitative, situated and based on an analysis of the *process* of consultancy in 12 different cases in different settings. Each case offers a systematic description of the way in which academic knowledge can be applied to solve practical challenges. The book has been written by researchers working in the field of intercultural communication, all involved in consultancy processes. The editors of the book decided to join forces as they are convinced that in many universities the added value of academic advice on intercultural communication is underestimated.

In this book, we use the terms *consultant* and *consultancy* in a broad sense. In case studies 1, 5, 6, 9 and 11, the emphasis is on a more traditional meaning of the consultant: an external organization has an issue they would like insight on; this organization commissions consultants to carry out research on the issue; the parties negotiate the work that needs to be done, bearing in mind costs and practicalities; the work is planned and then carried out maintaining ongoing contact and the outcome is evaluated. However, in academia, we are often positioned to do research when an information gap is noticed. Research is then carried out, and the findings are reported to those who are interested. Case studies 4 and 7 align with this form of consultancy. The purpose and the stakes of these forms of consultancy differ: in the first case, the consultation is commercial and negotiated, and in the other it is offered without having been requested. However, in both cases, the ultimate success of the consultation may be measured by the adoption or rejection of the advice.

The most difficult part of the consultancy process may be to truly understand what the client wishes to achieve. To be able to help an organization, a consultant must meet several requirements and understand the question of the organization, understand who plays a role in the advisory process, what is needed to conduct research, and present the results in a convincing way.

A consultant in *intercultural communication*, however, must meet additional requirements, which this book will address as well. Doing so, the following questions will be answered:

- What are the roles of intercultural consultants in achieving smooth and respectful communication between people with different cultural and language backgrounds?
- Given our extensive knowledge about the mechanisms of intercultural communication, how can we use this knowledge to contribute to the success of the organization in question?

Each example in this book is based on a real case in different international organization practices. For each case, the following stages are reviewed while adopting a variety of approaches to communication:

- We explore and try to understand a specific **intercultural (communication) situation**;
- We learn how the client's questions have been translated into a **research question**;
- We learn how the **data have been collected** to answer the research question;
- We learn how the research results have been translated to **answer the client's question**;
- We learn how the consultants have translated an intercultural problem into an **intercultural opportunity**;
- We **reflect critically** on the case, on the results that have been achieved, and on the factors that have influenced the adoption or rejection of the advice by the organization.

Even though languages and their collaterals (variety of languages, accents) are often seemingly the most prominent manifestations of multiculturality, the reader will discover that many other factors of social, historical, cultural and economic relevance also play a role in the situations that are described. Our goal, then, following Canagarajah (2013, p. 222), is to look beyond language to explore "the intercultural negotiation of agency," through the lens of enrichment in multiculturality. This means that we wish to move away from multiculturality as a problem to multiculturality as a resource.

How the Book Is Organized

The core of this book is formed by a detailed discussion of 12 different cases, each by a different author or team of authors. Many of the authors teach at university and/or work as consultants themselves. Each chapter covers the complete process of consultancy, from the first meeting with the client to the final stage of the process. In this way, for each case, the six points outlined earlier are reviewed. These real-life examples take the reader on a journey through Europe, Canada, the Antilles, Suriname and Saudi Arabia. We have tried to be as diverse as possible in the choice of the cases and to include all kinds of consultancy activities in different settings: educational and political settings, the business world, the academic world and non-governmental organizations.

Central questions guide the reader to the core challenges presented in each case. Additional questions for discussion and suggested readings are available as e-resources on the Routledge website. Also on the website is a Case

Study for Discussion for Part II – Case Study for Discussion: Educational Exchanges Between Dutch and Chinese Secondary Schools by Rosanne Severs and Roos Beerkens. These resources are provided to encourage readers to apply their new insights to the consultancy process, to explore additional documentation about the case, and to review additional literature. An index of keywords and authors, compiled by Emmy Gulikers, makes it possible to discover all kinds of links between the case studies.

Reference

Canagarajah, S. (2013). Agency and power in intercultural communication: Negotiating English in translocal spaces. *Language and Intercultural Communication, 13*(2), 202–224. doi:10.1080/14708477.2013.770867

2   Key Concepts

Roos Beerkens and Emmanuelle
Le Pichon-Vorstman

Increasing internationalization as well as digitalization have not only spurred encounters between people living in different parts of the world, but also the speed at which communication processes between these parties take place. Delegations of diplomats are a case in point. These are sent from one country to another with the mission to negotiate treaties and contracts. Typically, in earlier times, such missions could take months, and they can still take days to weeks at present. Initial exchanges of presents to break the ice, followed by culinary festivities, gradually usher in actual negotiations about the issue at hand. Nowadays, however, these elaborate, archetypal negotiations occur less frequently than before. Time pressure as well changes in communicative means have altered our conception of space and time in such a way that the chance to get to know each other prior to the actual negotiation is limited. There are different reasons for this evolution of which the two most important are:

1. Modern and digital tools that have not only greatly facilitated but also sped up the exchanges.
2. The individual groups of teams that have transitioned from homogeneous (sharing provenance, language and cultural background) to relatively heterogeneous. This implies that each team involved in an exchange is nowadays more likely to include individuals with a variety of cultural and knowledge backgrounds than was previously the case. Consequently, present-day teams are more likely to bring different and sometimes divergent funds of knowledge to the table.

These societal changes are likely at the root of a steep increase in the demand for intercultural communication consultants, which has, in fact, never been higher. There is, more than ever, a great need for consultancy in the context of intercultural communication.

Against this background, the first concept to investigate in this book is *communication*. Communication involves people in interaction, within a particular relationship, and within a particular context. Each exchange is influenced by local and global contexts, but also by the perception of reality by each participant. These perceptions may be fundamentally different, depending on cultural and knowledge backgrounds of the participants. When engaged in an interaction, in order to achieve smooth communication all participants need to negotiate their own perceptions to reach an understanding of the situation as perceived by others also engaged in the exchange. This negotiation of the communication process can be understood as a *continuum*, going from the ideal situation, where the understood purpose of the interaction is shared by the participants involved in the process, to a situation of communication breakdown when people do not understand each other (cf. Le Pichon-Vorstman, de Swart, Ceginskas, & van den Bergh, 2009). The more knowledge is shared between different parties in the exchange, the smoother the communication process.

The second concept that is key to this book is a compound of *inter* and *cultural*. If we are to investigate the process and outcomes of intercultural communication, we need to explain what we understand by both. We will start with the concept of culture, a concept that has been at the root of, and continues to incite, intense debates. On a side note, these debates are, in fact, themselves strongly influenced by some of the concepts that are at the core of this book. The objective of this book is not to reiterate such discussions. Rather, we wish to reposition this debate in its context to point out the differences between at least three of the movements and the vision supported within this book. Broadly speaking, these schools of thought have adopted a theoretical stand on culture which still influences the work of many consultants and the strategies they propose for intercultural communication. These ideas range from a static to an inherently dynamic view on culture:

1. *The essentialist view*, also called *national view*, considers culture as mainly static. In this view, individuals are grouped into a national identity that is both generalized and more or less fixed in the sense that it is supposed to be shared by the individuals who see themselves as members of this particular culture. One of the proponents of this view is Adler (1975). Adler defined the concept of culture as a perceptual frame of reference that a group may share, and which is influenced by members' orientation and worldview. Along the same lines, Hofstede (1983) defined cultures on the basis of dimensions that are deeply rooted in every culture and that can therefore be measured in each culture. Holliday, Hyde, and Kullman (2010) have described this definition of culture as

homogeneous. National borders form the divide between the supposed cultures. Inherent to this essentialist view is that it is highly normative or prescriptive. The latter implies that certain of these fixed generalizations are thought to be informative about effective communicative strategies. The approach is mainly quantitative.

2. In *the societal view* scholars narrow down the concept of culture to social groups, thinking beyond national borders (see for instance, Spencer-Oatey & Franklin, 2009; D'Iribarne, 1989). These authors claim that, within groups, people share some patterns of regularity, like orientations to life, values, principles and behavioural rituals (Spencer-Oatey & Franklin, 2009, p. 35), while differing on other aspects. According to Spencer-Oatey and Franklin, we all belong to multiple groups simultaneously (i.e. national or provincial provenance, religious groups, organizations, professional groups). Some scholars have attempted to classify these groups into different levels. Karahanna et al. distinguish a supranational level, which consists of, for instance, ethnic or religious cultures; a national level, where collective properties are attributed to citizens; a professional level, which entails social class and loyalty to the work industry; an organizational level, including the social and normative aspects that shape an organization; and a group level, constituted by individuals (van der Knaap, 2017; Karahanna, Evaristo, & Srite, 2006). In sum, this view expresses the need to identify the values supported by the groups involved.

3. A more *dynamic or interactionist view* describes culture as fluid, constantly changing and interactive movement (e.g. Dervin, 2012; Kim, 1988; ten Thije, 2016). According to Kim, culture is "a complex process of continuing interpretive activity internal to individuals as a result of their enculturation experiences" (1988, p. 48). Kim claims that it is through communication that we shape cultures (compare the essentialist view where culture shapes communication). According to this view, cultures are changing, adaptable, constituted in relation to others and constructed in discourse. This view is shared by, for instance Rampton (2006), who puts it in a slightly different way. To him, culture "emerges in people's activity together – it exists in the processes and resources involved in situated, dialogical, sense-making" (p. 20). Along the same lines the anthropologist Dettwyler sees cultures as negotiable and emergent depending on context (2011, p. 416). According to Abdallah-Pretceille (2003, p. 15) "cultures are less defined in terms of a sum of characteristics and cultural traits than in terms of relationships and interactions between individuals and groups." In these views, cultures are not simply a bundle of common values, norms, knowledge, resources, beliefs and behaviours, but they are constantly being made by many

different and varying aspects, among which nationality or ethnicity are only two of the influencing factors (Dettwyler, 2011, p. 416).

Interestingly, all of these conceptualizations affect the meaning that is assigned to *inter* in *intercultural communication*. To the first group of scholars, the prefix *inter* more or less equals *across*: communication across borders. For instance, what should a Dutch delegation expect when meeting a Chinese delegation? It is in a sense prescriptive. To the second group, *inter* refers to different groups and insists on the groups' cultures. For instance, how should a fusion between two different businesses be negotiated? Consultancy here often takes an ethnographic perspective since the answer can only be given after a thorough analysis of the culture of each group. To the third group of scholars, the culture of any exchange will be defined by its participants. The consultation will focus on each participant, taking into account their evolving identity perception, their belonging to multiple groups and the relationships that are established among the different partners: how can the inclusion of each participant be realized within a geographical space that is then reconceived as a shared meeting place?

If applied to intercultural consultancy, the prefix *inter* means that the consultants do not solely focus on communication between people from different linguistic or national cultural backgrounds, but that they observe, reflect, analyse communication between individuals who are part of different social (i.e. professional, organizational), historical (i.e. religious, regional, national) groups, and who at the same time reproduce and renew the culture to which they belong in interaction with others (Rampton, 2006). Cultures thus change over time and space, and are therefore hybrid and fluid. In this book we choose to go beyond the static, essentialist view of culture, even though we acknowledge that certain essentialist aspects cannot be avoided altogether and may even be informative. The danger of an essentialist view is not that it is incorrect but resides primarily in the temptation provided by its simplicity (stereotypes, ethnocentrism). When restricting oneself entirely to this view, one finds cultures become a given and cannot evolve interactively. The reality, however, is that people can. This is where the dynamic view of culture provides valuable input. This book can be viewed as eclectic, as the different authors discuss their views and strategies using elements from the different schools of thought summarized here.

Finally, we propose that the main objective of consultancy in intercultural communication is to provide discursive spaces to support the clients in exploring and understanding the different views of the participants involved, as well as of the influencing factors at stake in their interactions. With this knowledge in mind, the mission of the consultant is to help the client to reshape their understanding and strategies in order to reach their goal in an environment that favours "intercultural negotiation of agency" (see Canagarajah, 2013).

Position and Role of the Consultant

To help create a supportive, intercultural environment is one of the main tasks of an intercultural consultant. This has numerous implications, which distinguish a consultant in *inter*cultural communication from a regular consultant. Intercultural competences (see for instance, Spencer-Oatey & Franklin, 2009), knowledge about consultancy processes (cf. Ruck, 2009; Block, 2011; Cornelis, 2007; Van Ravenstein & Kok, 2014), and the consultant's own experiences are all relevant topics to explore. Therefore, in the case studies in this book, we start with the role and position of the consultant in intercultural communication, we then review the process of consultancy, and end with an explanation of the advice and what it means.

Consultants in the field of intercultural communication may adopt many different positions and roles. From freelancer, employee of a commercial consultancy agency, internal employee in a large organization, employee of a governmental consultancy, to academic consultant (employee at a university or research institute), and this list is not exhaustive. However, in this book we focus on the position of the *academic* consultant. When a university-educated consultant has to function in a non-academic environment, the person can find the consultancy process to be complicated. How should these consultants position themselves towards the profit requirement of a business or towards the political interest of a company? When faced with decisions that may impact the image of an enterprise or the political outcome of a societal issue, where does the consultant draw a line? And how does the consultant respond to a client begging a straightforward, practical solution, a recipe, for a recurrent problem? Is prescriptive or descriptive advice more suitable? In this book, the reader learns that in some situations academic consultants may opt for descriptive advice, providing an academic perspective on the situation and research-based insights, whereas in other situations, they might need to lean towards a prescriptive or normative advice, when a more persuasive form of consultancy is called for.

Tasks of Consultants in Intercultural Communication

If we believe that culture is dynamic, fluid and interactive, we accept that our cultures are constantly re-constructed and co-constructed. The identity of the consultant and the identities of all participants in the exchange are impacted by the situations of intercultural communication. In fact, most of the work of intercultural advisers concerns understanding and mediating the norms, cultural values, ideologies and power relationships of all participants, including the norms, values and ideologies of the adviser. Therefore, each intercultural adviser deals with rich and vulnerable situations of communication in which everyone is modified by the process. For instance, our analysis of the situation and advice will often imply a shift in the positional identities of the clients. It is important, however, to remain wary of researcher bias. The essentialist view of culture is always tempting as it panders to our own ethnocentric positioning. In other words, neutrality is a myth. As stated by Ogay and Edelmann (2016):

> The way for a reasonable understanding of culture and cultural difference is narrow and it is easy to fall into the traps of culturalisation and indifference. . . . The metaphors of culture (as language, air and non-Newtonian fluid) are helpful to foster an understanding of culture as indispensable yet at the same time unseizable. The dialectical square of cultural difference helps to put words on the contradictions and tensions experienced in intercultural situations. It helps to understand how short-sighted either-or choices are and to accept the dialectical tension between equality and diversity.
>
> (p. 397)

Because the work of the intercultural consultant is about "put[ting] words on the contradictions and tensions experienced in intercultural situations" (2016, p. 397), the first step of consultancy is to understand the situation at hand in its specificity. We believe that no two identical cases exist and recipes for consultancy do not exist either. All cases are unique and dynamic. Therefore, it is of primary importance for the consultant to understand the situation as well as possible before even entering on the process of consultancy.

In this book, we focus on the perspective of the client, starting with the request for advice and then working towards that advice – often provisional – while leveraging professional and academic expertise. While the core of the advice to the client relies on the consultant's expertise in intercultural communication, successful transfer of knowledge can only be achieved through successful communication with the client. We therefore insist on the communicative process of consultancy. In the end, the success of a consultancy process is not measured by the solidity of the advice offered, but by the extent to which the advice is adopted by the client.

References

Abdallah-Pretceille, M. (2003). *Former et éduquer en contexte hétérogène. Pour un humanisme du divers*. Paris: Antropos.

Adler, P. (1975). The transitional experience: An alternative view of culture shock. *Journal of Humanistic Psychology*, *15*(4), 13–23.

Block, P. (2011). *Flawless consulting: A guide to getting your expertise used*. San Francisco, CA: Pfeiffer.

Canagarajah, S. (2013). Agency and power in intercultural communication: Negotiating English in translocal spaces. *Language and Intercultural Communication*, *13*(2), 202–224. doi:10.1080/14708477.2013.770867

Cornelis, L. (2007). *Adviseren met perspectief: rapporten en presentaties maken*. Bussum: Coutinho.

Dervin, F. (2012). Cultural identity, representation and othering. In Jane Jackson (Ed.), *The Routledge handbook of language and intercultural communication* (Vol. 2, pp. 181–194). London: Routledge. https://doi.org/10.4324/9780203805640

Dettwyler, K. A. (2011). *Cultural anthropology & human experience: The feast of life*. Long Grove, IL: Waveland Press, Inc.

D'Iribarne, P. (1989). *La logique de l'honneur: Gestion des entreprises et traditions nationales*. Paris: Seuil.

Hofstede, G. (1983). National Cultures Revisited. *Behavior Science Research*, *18*(4), 285–305. https://doi.org/10.1177/106939718301800403

Holliday, A., Hyde, M., & Kullman, J. (2010). *Intercultural communication: An advanced resource book for students*. New York, NY: Routledge.

Karahanna, E., Evaristo, J. R., & Srite, M. (2006). Levels of culture and individual behavior: An integrative perspective. *Advanced Topics in Global Information Management*, *5*(1), 30–50.

Kim, Y. Y. (1988). *Communication and cross-cultural adaptation: An integrative theory*. Clevedon and Philadelphia: Multilingual Matters.

Le Pichon-Vorstman, E., de Swart, H., Ceginskas, V., & van den Bergh, H. (2009). Language learning experience in school context and metacognitive awareness of multilingual children. *International Journal of Multilingualism*, *6*(3), 256–280.

Ogay, T., & Edelmann, D. (2016). 'Taking culture seriously': Implications for intercultural education and training. *European Journal of Teacher Education*, *39*(3), 388–400. doi:10.1080/02619768.2016.1157160

Rampton, B. (2006). *Language in late modernity interaction in an urban school*. Cambridge: Cambridge University Press.

Ruck, B. (2009). *Overtuigend adviseren. De juiste vragen stellen, begrijpelijk schrijven, boeiend presenteren*. Den Haag: Academic Service.

Spencer-Oatey, H., & Franklin, P. (2009). *Intercultural interaction: A multidisciplinary approach to intercultural communication*. New York, NY: Palgrave Macmillan.

ten Thije, J. D. (2016). Intercultural communication. In L. Jäger, W. Holly, P. Krapp, & S. Weber (Eds.), *Sprach – Kultur – Kommunikation/Language – culture – communication. Ein internationales Handbuch zu Linguistik als Kulturwissenschaft. An international handbook of linguistics as cultural study* (pp. 581–594). Berlin: Mouton de Gruyter.

van der Knaap, D. (2017). *Expat life: Experiences of expats living in the Netherlands, an exploration of the experiences of expats in terms of culture shock and adjustment* (Unpublished master's thesis). Utrecht University, Utrecht, The Netherlands.

Van Ravenstein, I., & Kok, G. (2014). *IC in 3D*. Amsterdam: Adfo Groep.

Part I
Policymakers

Case Study 1

Advising Municipalities on Schooling Newly Arrived Migrant Pupils

Emmanuelle Le Pichon-Vorstman
and Sergio Baauw

The Case

In 2014, a board member of a primary school in a large city in the Netherlands approached the authors with a request for consultancy. The specific question concerned the evaluation of a primary school that welcomes newly arrived migrant pupils. This request was an interesting one as its intercultural aspects touched upon the very topical and highly political issue of inclusion of pupils and families with different languages and cultures into the Dutch school system. We immediately responded positively because we had just completed an international project on the inclusion of inheritance language pupils in Europe and we were eager to explore the same issues at a national level. According to our contact, the school board approached us because the municipality wished to evaluate the effects of the financial support provided to the education of these newly arrived pupils in the city. The situation was urgent since the subsidy scheme was coming to an end. In fact, municipalities are required to provide regular reports to the Dutch government evaluating locally managed projects and their efficiency when these projects are funded by the national government. We agreed to submit a research proposal to the municipality within two weeks.

At the primary school level, the organization of the education of newly arrived pupils in the Netherlands is taken care of by the local authorities. The organization of the system is thus characterized by decentralization. This implies that every municipality receives a certain amount of earmarked governmental funding, but can decide independently how this financial support will be spent to further the education of newly arrived students. Consequently, the organizational structure of the education can vary considerably between different cities. In our case, the city set up a separate school specialized in the reception of newly arrived primary and pre-primary school pupils. Accordingly, all newly arrived pupils are automatically registered for this separate school upon their arrival. After approximately one year at this school, the pupils leave to join a mainstream primary school, usually in their own neighborhood. To illustrate the diversity in local policies in this regard: another major city in the Netherlands did not choose to establish a special school but instead offers reception classes in regular schools. Similar to our city, pupils generally attend these special classes for one year. Municipalities that use the latter system tend to select schools to develop expertise in this matter, which means that pupils may be directed towards a school that is not in their district.

Decentralization can be an asset for the educational system, especially when it comes to the reception of newly arrived students: as the influx is unpredictable, this system may provide the flexibility and adaptability that is needed to cope with changing circumstances and adapt optimally to a local situation. However, when it comes to their *inclusion*, decentralization may also have its downsides. For instance, in a decentralized system, schools have more autonomy regarding the content of instruction, thus to adjust the curriculum to the need of their pupils (Dumcius, Nicaise, Balcaite, Huttova, & Siarova, 2012); however, newly arrived migrant pupils are highly mobile even after their arrival. Moving to another city, the pupils will thus have to adjust to yet another study programme. This makes the continuity of educational trajectory of these pupils even more challenging. From this perspective, it is clear that the research we were commissioned to carry out would not only be relevant to the municipality in question. The issues we were asked to explore were also likely to be relevant to newly arrived families and their children, the school and its employees, and ultimately, the Dutch society and government. The municipality's motivation in commissioning our research was clear. Its main goal was to obtain reliable information about the situation to guide policymakers in finding solutions to existing problems and enable these pupils to enjoy the best possible education. Our report would provide an assessment of its current policy with recommendations for the future and provide insight into the concerns expressed by the school board. Our input would help the city to obtain continued government support, and perhaps, although this was not formulated explicitly, to reduce the costs.

Description of the Research Design

After a number of calls with a city council representative and discussions with the school board, we formulated the following questions:

1. How is the separate primary school for newly arrived pupils doing in terms of efficiency?
2. In what ways can the current educational system for newly arrived pupils be improved?

The next step consisted of the translation of these questions into research goals. We decided that the research should focus on the development of the pupils during their stay in the separate primary school.

As indicated previously, we were instructed that the research could not exceed one school year, and we were therefore obliged to omit several potentially relevant subjects. For instance, we decided not to study the effect of the transition(s) many newly arrived pupils undergo when moving from the special school to a mainstream school. We were also unable to compare the effects of this city's policy to those of organizational structures in other cities. This would have required the collection of data in other cities, which was beyond the scope and budget of this assignment. In addition, between cities there are important differences in the newly arrived populations. This extreme heterogeneity in terms of age upon arrival, country of provenance, and previous education makes even a tentative comparison precarious. A research protocol was written and sent to the client, as well as a budget and a contract. After some time, the client called and asked us to reconsider the protocol and expand the scope. To this purpose, we needed one more school year and we thus reworked the proposal, adding a year to the budget, and an extra research question on transitions to the protocol. This allowed us to expand the initial question to include the aspect of transition: How do the pupils adapt to the regular school system after having left the special school in terms of school achievement?

Results of European research on migrant pupils' school achievements underline the underachievement of this population (PISA, Dumcius et al., 2012) and a higher risk on early school dropout (Fan & Wolters, 2014). In addition, studies from Canada and the United States of America show that pupils need at least five years in the educational system before they are on a par with their monolingual peers. However, these studies do not reflect the high diversity of newly arrived students that European schools are confronted with. There is thus a lack of research on the school achievements of newly arrived migrant pupils in this particular context, resulting in a lack of insight into the ways in which their needs can be addressed more effectively.

Once we reached agreement on budget and protocol, we formed a working group around the researchers in which all stakeholders were represented: the municipality, the school board, the school principal and staff, the other school boards of the municipality, and the researchers. Meetings were scheduled approximately four times a year and were meant to inform the parties about the research in progress, to discuss ongoing issues, and to make sure that we would base our advice on existing resources. When formulating advice, it is essential to identify solutions that are available within the immediate context of the client to avoid solutions that are out of the client's reach (see for instance, Ruck, 2009). The importance of the meetings, therefore, cannot be overestimated. For one, solutions and answers to the questions that came up during the meetings were very often provided by the actors themselves who, ultimately, have a better knowledge of the situation than we do. For instance, teachers knew the daily routine in the classroom and they were the ones who explained it to us. Without their knowledge and collaboration, researchers could not have made progress. Teachers also had solutions to their problems within the school, for instance, a staff member who spoke the language of some of the pupils and who could be hired to act as an intermediary for communication with the pupils' relatives. However, these potential solutions may have been underexploited and need an exterior evaluator to be identified. Second, these regular meetings helped maintain sufficient transparency in the research process. In fact, the future of the school and of its workers partly depended on the outcome of the research. Therefore, the research and the researchers could be perceived as a threat for the school and staff instead of as support. On the other hand, the success of the research also depended on the school's willingness to participate. Our expectation was that only if we somehow managed to maintain optimal communication between school and researchers would both parties benefit fully from the knowledge held by those involved. Third, researchers may come across issues that can already be addressed during the research period. This underlines the value of the consultancy not only as a means to generate an end product in the form of advice, but also as a productive process in itself. The following example may help to illustrate this point. During the first year of research, we consulted the website of the school. We came to the conclusion that it was unclear at what audience the website was targeted. For instance, all the information was in Dutch, a language that most newly arrived parents would not be able to read. Some information on the site was relevant to the parents and relatives, some to the city council, some to the pupils themselves. However, the information was difficult to find and not categorized according to potential readers, for example information about the school days, about the classroom life, about the administration around it, about the financial issues. Bringing this issue up in one of the regular meetings was enough to encourage the school to revise the website to better match it with the target readership.

Thus, two research questions remained that needed answering: How do the pupils develop (1) *during* and (2) *after* their stay in the separate primary school? By answering these questions, we expected to answer the initial questions of the municipality: How is the special school for newly arrived pupils doing in terms of efficiency? In what ways can the currently implemented schooling system for newly arrived pupils be improved?

Our research was based on both qualitative and quantitative methods. We recruited 50 pupils aged 5 to 11. We measured the development of second language understanding and production and gathered information about personality and behavioural development. We also conducted semi-structured, in-depth interviews with school management and teachers, obtained information through questionnaires filled in by teachers, and collected data from the school database. In addition, we traced former pupils of the programme to analyse their school careers.

Consultancy and Acceptance

The results had to be converted into intervention management. Of course, this step usually requires interpretation of the research results and therefore is subject to discussion and negotiation. The most important result was positive: pupils developed well during their stay in the special classroom and were very soon on a par with classroom peers after their stay in that classroom even though there is a growing remaining achievement gap with age peers (Le Pichon-Vorstman, Baauw & Vorstman, 2016). The results could be summarized in the following way:

1. The trajectory of newly arrived pupils is very complex and does not end once a pupil has entered the Netherlands. Discontinuity is the main challenge in the education of these pupils.
2. Heterogeneous experiences of previous schooling and potential traumatizing experiences considerably complicate the child's ability to adjust to (any) situation, including a new school setting and should be addressed as soon as possible.

Results were discussed in detail in the working group as well as individually with the different stakeholders. Based on these discussions, we formulated several recommendations:

1. In order to prevent discontinuity of schooling and to assure faster comprehension and access to knowledge for all pupils, we recommended the implementation of a school language policy in the school, in particular one that would include the languages of the pupils;
2. In order to allow teachers to focus more on individual levels of pupils we recommended:
   a. the introduction of one extra expert teacher per classroom; investment in continued professionalization of the teachers and school staff;
   b. the implementation of a programme for the well-being of the pupils targeting pupils with possible traumas;
   c. more hand-in-hand collaboration with specialized institutions.

The results had different consequences for different stakeholders: schools, school boards, city council, or even the Ministry of Education. For instance, questions that were raised during the discussions were:

- What does the school need from the municipality to better address the mental well-being of the pupils during their stay in the reception classroom?
- What do regular schools need from the reception school to facilitate the transition of the pupils?
- What does the school need to teach the teachers to foster the pupils' own languages in order to boost the cognitive and emotional development of the pupils?

As mentioned at the beginning of this chapter, this consultancy touched upon the very topical and highly political issues of inclusion of pupils and families with different languages and cultures into the Dutch school system. Therefore, the process of negotiation also implied a confrontation between stakeholders' opinions and research outcomes. For instance, our recommendation of including the languages of the pupils in the classroom routine met with some reluctance given the financial consequences of such policy. This is understandable in light of the fact that financial support from the government for pupils' own languages as teaching medium in schools was abrogated in the Netherlands in 2004. It was important to discuss these issues in the working groups and to explain the value of the pupils' culture (with language being a core value) and its implications for the cognitive and emotional development of the children based on our findings and scholarly literature.

Interestingly, this case confirms the added value of academic research in comparison to independent consultancy agencies. In choosing academic research, clients know that there is an (often implicit) claim for independence, that research protocols will be subject to evaluation by an independent ethics committee, that the results will be further analysed, and that the answer to the initial request may not necessarily please the client. This tension between research outcome and political pressure for certain interpretations should be acknowledged and compels researchers to stay alert and be wary of any politically motivated interpretation of their results. To stimulate best practice in this regard, optimal intercultural communication (including interdisciplinary communication) should be one of the targets of the whole consultancy process from the very beginning. In this case, recommendations were presented as potential options to improve the situation. All recommendations were written with the consent of the three main stakeholders: the city council, the school boards, and the school staff. Successful intercultural management is a process that needs to be continuously negotiated and based on mutual trust between client, stakeholders, and researchers.

References

Dumcius, R., Nicaise, I., Balcaite, I., Huttova, J., & Siarova, H. (2012). *Study on educational support for newly arrived migrant children.* Final report prepared for the European Commission. Luxembourg: Publications Office of the European Union.

European Commission. (2015). *Language learning and teaching in multilingual classrooms.* Retrieved from http://ec.europa.eu/languages/policy/learning-languages/multilingual-classrooms_en.htm

Fan, W., & Wolters, C. A. (2014). School motivation and high school dropout: The mediating role of educational expectation. *British Journal of Educational Psychology, 84*(1), 22–39.

Le Pichon-Vorstman, E., Baauw, S., & Vorstman, J. (2016, August). *School development of newly arrived migrant pupils in the Netherlands at primary school level.* Paper presented at ECER Conference, Dublin, Ireland.

Ruck, B. (2009). *Overtuigend adviseren. De juiste vragen stellen, begrijpelijk schrijven, boeiend presenteren.* Den Haag: Academic Service.

Case Study 2

Intercultural Communication Between a Municipality and Polish Migrants

Daria van Kolck (Boruta) and Paulina Wołoszyn

The Case

Since economic expansion of the common European market has enabled easy movement of humans and human capital, new cross-cultural and linguistic relations appear in many regions (Cornips, De Rooij, & Stengs, 2017). Although so-called peripheral areas in Europe also have to deal with the cultural and linguistic consequences of the movement of people and goods, they are not often discussed in the literature (Wang et al., 2014). The following case shows that intercultural movement not only creates challenges for local and rural communities in the periphery, but also offers opportunities for solving problems.

An interesting example of long-standing cultural and linguistic diversity is the Dutch province of Limburg. Due to the coal mines in the south-east which triggered economic migrants from Eastern (and Southern) Europe from the beginning of the 20th century, Limburg has a long migration history. In Limburg members from diverse cultural and ethnic backgrounds have been living together from the beginning of the 20th century (Cornips, 2013; Wang et al., 2014; Cornips et al., 2017). In the 1970s the coal mines were closed, but their impact on the cultural and linguistic diversity in that region was significant. Thirty years later a new influx of migrants from Eastern Europe, including Poland, opened a new chapter in the intercultural and multilingual experience of this province.

The number of Polish migrants in the Netherlands has significantly increased over the past 15 years. The accession of Poland to the European Union in 2004, entitling people with Polish nationality to work without a work permit from 2007 onwards, facilitated the circulation of people and goods between Poland and other European countries. One of its consequences is an increase in the number of Polish labour migrants, who come to the Netherlands because of the economic advantages (CBS, 2016 in Wołoszyn, 2017a, p. 5). Labour migrants move abroad for the purpose of employment and remain there for a certain period, for example for seasonal work (Ooijevaar, Sluiter, & Verschuren, 2013). In the Netherlands labour migrants increasingly decide to settle, however (Ooijevaar et al., 2013). Especially in North Limburg, there are many labour migrants and 90% of these migrants come from Poland ("Het belang van arbeidsmigranten," 2016). As the local youngsters from Limburg move to the *Randstad*, the metropolitan region in the centre of the country, the economic and social structure of many peripheral municipalities has experienced changes, encountering brain draining and aging processes (Cornips et al., 2017). The Polish and East European migrants provide necessary labour, especially for the agricultural sector in many municipalities in North Limburg. Some of these municipalities are explicitly opting for the group of Polish migrants, as they realized the importance of the Poles for a vital social life and economy of their local communities.

These municipalities therefore attach high priority to communicating effectively with this group of new residents. Societal institutions like health care, administration or education constitute "potential spaces of multilingualism" (Rehbein, 2013, pp. 51, 70) with a need to communicate in more than one language. They are described as "potential" because multilingual communication does not happen spontaneously. Local governments are an example of spaces where particular tendencies towards multilingualism can be observed. Local governments have to transfer information to newly arrived migrants: they have to be informed of their rights, of what they have to arrange after their arrival or where they could look for help in case of problems. To improve their communication with migrants, local governments can take such measures as preparing informative brochures in the migrants' language, translating important information on their website(s) or organizing language courses for migrants (Porila & ten Thije, 2008).

Two studies have been set up to examine intercultural communication processes between two municipalities in a peripheral area in the Netherlands, namely Horst aan de Maas and Peel en Maas in Limburg and its Polish migrants. The project was a joined initiative of the Meertens Instituut (MI) in Amsterdam, Utrecht University (UU), the Institute for Transnational and Euregional Cross Border Cooperation and Mobility (ITEM) at Maastricht University (UM).[1]

The Research Process

The studies by Boruta (2015) and Wołoszyn (2017a) were carried out over a period of three months and data for their analyses were collected during one month of ethnographic fieldwork. Their analyses were conducted on the basis of notes from (participant) observation, unstructured and semistructured interviews, photographs and sound recordings. In ethnographic studies the researcher describes a culture from the inside (emic) perspective (Boeije, 2005) made possible through fieldwork conducted within a community. As the researcher observes and participates in the daily activities of residents, (s)he also slowly becomes a (distant) member of the community. Boruta (2015) and Wołoszyn (2017a) observed the daily life of the Polish residents of the municipalities, especially in shops and Polish consultancy agencies.[2] The researchers also took an active part in workshops and projects organized for Polish migrants and attended meetings of an advisory group of the municipalities for Polish residents. Additionally, to reach as many Polish migrant workers as possible, Wołoszyn (2017a) conducted a survey in a Polish shop and a Polish consultancy agency. The aim of the questionnaire was to find out whether the information about customs and rules in the Netherlands provided by the municipalities was effective for Polish migrants working and living in Dutch society, and whether the Polish migrants could indeed find this information.

The aim of the first pilot research (Boruta, 2015) was to describe the linguistic and cultural interaction of the Polish and local communities in the municipality of Horst aan de Maas. Using participant observation, information was obtained about the backgrounds of the (young) Polish and local residents, career opportunities, plans for the future and attitudes of the Polish and local community. In ethnographic research, data collection is a cyclic process: conclusions drawn from participant observation during the fieldwork are shared and discussed with the parties involved. Therefore, in March 2016, the conclusions of the ethnographic research of Boruta were presented at the annual conference at Statistics Netherlands (CBS) in Heerlen, where, among others, the city council and the police from Horst aan de Maas were present.[3] The governmental representatives showed their interest in more specific research which could provide insight in the interactions with the Poles living in Horst aan de Maas. Leonie Cornips remained in contact with the relevant parties and a year later, in February 2017, Paulina Wołoszyn set up the next sociolinguistic research in commission of the municipality and police of Horst aan de Maas and Peel en Maas, in cooperation with Utrecht University and the Meertens Instituut.

In the second study, Wołoszyn looked for practical solutions to improve the communication and mutual understanding between the Polish residents of Horst aan de Maas and Peel en Maas on the one hand and local governments on the other (Wołoszyn, 2017a). In this research Wołoszyn (2017a) focused on communication as well as information transfer between the police, municipality and Polish immigrants. The police team wanted to know what information the Polish migrant workers need, if the provided information reaches the Polish immigrants and if not, how they want to be informed by the local institutions. The police team also wanted to find out if the Polish immigrants are open to social integration with the local residents and how they view the police and the Dutch municipal institutions. These questions were converted into a research goal. The aim of the research was to find out how the communication between local governments and Polish immigrants could be improved. A plan was presented and discussed with the police team and a municipality representative in Horst two months before the start of the research.

Both studies showed that the initiatives taken by different local institutions point to a need for and interest in creating space for contacts between Polish and local residents of Horst aan de Maas. Examples of such activities are the language tandem project "het Koempel project," Polish musicians who performed together with the local orchestra, and a Polish-Dutch culinary weekend (Boruta, 2015). The Polish-Dutch dialogue is also visible in the linguistic landscape in the municipality. In the public space a great deal of information in Polish can be observed (see Pictures 2.1, 2.2 and 2.3).

The language difference is usually believed to be one of the biggest obstacles for the officials of the municipality to communicate effectively with the migrants. While this is true, there are also other factors which need to be taken into consideration, such as the diversity within the groups of migrants who

Picture 2.1 A Poster in Polish (English: Are you looking for a good book? Now you can borrow Polish books at BiblioNu) at the Entrance of the Library [30 April 2015]

Picture 2.2 Dutch and Polish Texts (English: Almost for free) Observed at the Jumble Sale [3 May 2015]

English Translation Below

If you live in the Netherlands, you should know this!

The Maximum Speed in Residential Areas is 50 km per Hour and on Motorways 130 km per hour.

If you exceed the allowed speed, it may cost you from € 26 to more than € 2000.

Driving Under the Influence of Alcohol is a Crime and is Punished as a Crime

Driving under the influence of alcohol (depending on the result of the examination) is fined at least 300€. Please note that your driving license may be also seized by the authorities.

Refusal or obstruction during alcohol measuring in the body is treated as a crime and always leads to the highest penalty.

Driving without fastened safety belts €140.

Driving on the red light €230.

Talking on the phone without a speakerphone while driving € 230.

Picture 2.3 The Information Board in the Centre of Horst With the Poster Inside [25 April 2015]

Maladjustment to Road Signs

Parking the car in a forbidden place €90.
No entry €140.
Traffic ban €90.

Local City Law

Dealing with physiological needs in public places €140.
Drinking alcohol or carrying open cans/bottles of alcohol in some
   parts of the city (for example in the city centre) €90.

Please Note

Anyone who has attained 14 years is required to present an identity
document at the request of a police officer or a city guard.

Picture 2.3 Continued

are often seen as one, homogeneous group (Spencer-Oatey & Franklin, 2009). The pilot research of Boruta showed that the Polish community in Horst aan de Maas was heterogeneous as well. There are "seasonal migrants," who come to the Netherlands for a few months to perform seasonal work in addition to "temporary migrants," who constantly switch between Poland and the Netherlands, and who come to Limburg from time to time or they live there for the larger part of the year (Boruta, 2015, p. 31). Finally, there are also the "permanent" migrants, who settle in the Netherlands and who admit openly that they do not plan to go back to Poland although in practice it is often very difficult to distinguish permanent migrants from the temporary ones (Boruta, 2015, p. 34). Age and future orientation are the most important factors among the Poles in their openness about their integration in the local community.

   Boruta (2015) observed some cultural clashes in contacts between Polish and Dutch residents. For instance, posters prepared by the police and translated by the police officers from Poland who cooperate with the Dutch police might have presented a Polish immigrant as someone who is not welcome. However, during the second stage of the research, interviews with Polish migrants showed that none of the respondents experienced the poster as insulting. It was concluded that the text does not necessarily refer to cultural background and cultural differences, and that its interpretation can differ per person, depending on who is interpreting and in what context.

Consultancy and Acceptance

The results of Wołoszyn's (2017a) study show that a great deal of information is translated into Polish and available to Polish immigrants in the municipalities, such as brochures and flyers about healthcare in the Netherlands, about the Dutch educational system or Dutch language courses (Wołoszyn, 2017a). Unfortunately, these informative folders often do not reach the target group. The local governments seem to communicate with Polish immigrants in a way that does not have the immigrants' preference. First, the information does not seem to be spread in places where Polish migrants can easily find it. The research shows that the Polish migrants who settle in the Netherlands or stay there for more than a few months look for information on the Internet, where the folders in Polish are difficult to find. Moreover, the flyers are not available in all Polish shops or consultancy offices in the region and even if they are, they are often not up to date (Wołoszyn, 2017a). However, while the Internet is a perfect solution for the permanent Polish residents, not all the Polish migrants have Internet access. To this group belong temporary and seasonal migrants who live very often on campsites where there is little or no Internet connection. Moreover, they are rarely not registered in the municipality. These groups of migrants usually complete the necessary formalities through their temporary employment agencies and receive information there. Hence, these migrants can be approached most efficiently by the employment agencies or their employees (Wołoszyn, 2017a).

Polish migrants also need to know more about the tasks of the municipality and the police. To give an example: Polish migrants do not know that the municipality includes regional teams which are responsible for youth care, work and care for the long-term sick and elderly residents of the municipality (Wołoszyn, 2017a). Their aim is to respond to questions of residents and to find solutions for their problems. Polish migrants hardly ever take their questions to the town hall or the police office. In Poland official institutions are often seen as slow and inefficient and the last instance to turn to with questions. The interviews with the Polish respondents showed that Polish migrants are also often unaware of what kind of help they can get from the local governments (Wołoszyn, 2017a). They simply do not know what possibilities and rights they have.

Based on the results of both researchers, advice has been formulated for the police team in both municipalities as well as for the local governments. The main recommendations were:

- to create a website in Polish or to translate into Polish the most important pieces of information for migrants on the website of the local governments;

- more communication and collaboration between the local governments and employment agencies so that more temporary Polish immigrants can be reached;
- to supply all the Polish shops and consultancy offices for Polish immigrants in the municipality with informative brochures, brochures and folders need to be updated as well;
- to spread information about the role and duties of the municipality and the police;
- to support projects that are focused on integration.

The research set-up, process, results and the advice were presented in September 2017 at the city hall in Horst by Wołoszyn. The advice was widely discussed and the local representatives were eager to improve the Polish website and to adjust the folders. It is worth mentioning that the presentation also raised many questions. The results of the research had consequences not only for the main stakeholders: the local government, the police and the Polish immigrants, but also for the employment agencies, consultancy offices and the owners of the Polish shops. In fact, all these stakeholders have different interests. The main purpose of the local government is to inform new residents about Dutch law and regulations since the newly arrived residents need to follow the rules and know their rights in the Netherlands. The employment agencies, on the other hand, have to acquire as many workers as possible at the lowest possible cost. They often see no advantage in informing people about their rights or other work. In consequence, the collaboration between the government and employment agencies can be problematic. In the creation of an intercultural dialogue within the municipality the guidance of an intercultural specialist can be of great assistance (Boruta, 2015; Wołoszyn, 2017a).

The summaries of both reports were shared with the key members of the local community, such as social workers, civil servants and Polish and Dutch residents of the municipality who took part in the researches. Afterwards, the findings from both studies were published in the regional newspaper in columns by Leonie Cornips.[4]

Half a year after the final presentation of the second research in September 2017, the researchers contacted a representative from the municipality to find out if the advice had been implemented. It emerged that a 100% increase of labour migrants was expected for 2018 because of the great demand for workers from the logistics sector. That is why the issue of effective communication with the labour migrants is still important. In the six months following the research, the leaflets had been updated and there were new brochures about obtaining financial contributions for children, obtaining a bicycle or a laptop for school. The advisory group still meet every six weeks.

The members now discuss the option of the municipality to hire someone who speaks Polish. The municipality is still planning to implement further advice such as increasing availability of the leaflets and making them easier to find on the municipality website.

Final Reflection

A key role in both projects was played by scholars of the Meertens Instituut, Utrecht University, and Institute for Transnational and Euregional Cross Border Cooperation and Mobility (ITEM) at Maastricht University. They offered supervision, knowledge and expertise. Leonie Cornips as an expert on the language and culture in Limburg provided both students with a deeper understanding of the research area. Furthermore, Cornips and Hans Schmeets (Statistics Netherlands/UM) took care of the funding of the project within ITEM, which made the first part of the research possible. Finally, thanks to the close cooperation and contacts between the scholars and the local government after the pilot project in 2015, the municipality expressed its interest in follow-up research, which was set up in 2017 and partly financed by the local government.

The process of the intercultural mediation was an enriching experience for both researchers as well as the community. The researchers gained insights in the Polish community in the Netherlands, which they are to a certain extent a part of. Boruta (2015) and Wołoszyn (2017b) mention their special position as researchers during the fieldwork. As participating observants, the researchers were both insiders and outsiders among the Polish residents of the researched municipalities. Wołoszyn (2017b) admitted that it was difficult for her to address foreign people in Polish stores: "I have noticed that Polish residents are suspicious. I often felt like an outsider there. During my first day I heard from a shop assistant 'I was surprised when you said 'dzień dobry' [good morning], you are different from the other Poles here. You have a different face, you wear different clothes, you behave also differently.' I had this feeling of 'being different' very often, so at first it was difficult for me to earn trust of Polish people there. On the other hand, after a few weeks I became friends with some respondents, they invited me for a coffee, we went also to a pub. At a certain point it was difficult to keep distance and to remember your role in doing research" (Wołoszyn, 2017b, p. 12).

The double perspective of the researchers went together with their "double loyalty" to members of the local community and to the Poles. An example of this would be the local orchestra organizing an annual event at the end of the summer. Boruta was invited for an organizational meeting before the event together with the musicians and the Poles. That year the musicians wanted to perform in the local church where the Polish parish is located. The show was a combination of music and dance and the group was planning to ask the approval of the Polish pastor. During the meeting a discussion arose about the dancing. Dancing in a church is not common practice within the Polish community – the Poles consider a church as a sacred place and dancing can be considered disrespectful. The researcher mediated between the parties, who both wanted to solve this situation. Moreover, the researcher, as someone who is involved in the local and the Polish community, felt obliged to show each the perspective of the other.

Notes

1. The research was supervised by Leonie Cornips (Meertens Instituut/UM), who specializes in "Language culture in Limburg" and Jan D. ten Thije (Utrecht University).
2. Personal consulting offices which are run by Polish people who live in the Netherlands a few or more years and are well oriented in the Netherlands. Polish immigrants who cannot speak Dutch or just arrived in the Netherlands can get information and help there regarding, among others, translating letters, filing a tax return, taking out health insurance or registering with the municipality.
3. The conference was organized by Hans Schmeets and Leonie Cornips on March 31, 2016.
4. "Pools in Horst," *De Limburger*, 14 December 2015; "Taalbarrières," *De Limburger*, 29 February 2016; "Intercultureel," *De Limburger*, 27 November 2017.

References

Boeije, H. (2005). Kwalitatief onderzoek. Dataverzamelingsmethoden. In H. 't Hart & H. Boeije (Eds.), *Onderzoeksmethoden* (pp. 261–274). Amsterdam: Boom onderwijs.
Boruta, D. (2015). *Etnografisch onderzoek naar de Poolse gemeenschap in Horst aan de Maas in het kader van taalcultuurstudie*. Amsterdam and Utrecht: Meertens Instituut, Universiteit Utrecht.
Cornips, L. (2013). Taalcultuur: Talen in beweging. *Taal & Tongval, 3*, 125–147.
Cornips, L., De Rooij, V., & Stengs, I. (2017). Carnivalesque language use and the construction of local identities: A plea for language culture as a field of research. *Jahrbuch für Europäische Ethnologie. Die Niederlande, 12*(3), 61–90.
Het belang van arbeidsmigranten. (2016). *Arbeidsmigranten zijn welkom*. Retrieved from www.horstaandemaas.nl/Ondernemers/Vergunningen_en_regelingen/Slotdocument_Het_belang_van_arbeidsmigranten
Ooijevaar, J., Sluiter, N., & Verschuren, S. (2013). *Bevolkingstrends 2013. Immigranten en werknemers uit de Europese Unie in Nederland*. Den Haag: Centraal Bureau voor de Statistiek.
Porila, A., & ten Thije, J. D. (2008). Ämter und Behörden. In J. Straub, A. Weidemann, & D. Weidemann (Hrsg.), *Handbuch interkulturelle Kommunikation und Kompetenz* (pp. 699–707). Stuttgart: Metzler.
Rehbein, J. (2013). The future of multilingualism: Towards a HELIX of societal multilingualism under global auspices. In K. Bührig & B. Meyer (Eds.), *Transferring*

linguistic know-how into institutional practice (pp. 43–72). Amsterdam and Philadelphia: John Benjamins Publishing Company.

Spencer-Oatey, H., & Franklin, P. (2009). *Intercultural interaction: A multidisciplinary approach to intercultural communication*. Basingstoke: Palgrave Macmillan.

Wang, X., Spotti, M., Juffermans, K., Cornips, L., Kroon, S., & Blommaert, J. (2014). Globalization in the margins: Toward a re-evaluation of language and mobility. *Applied Linguistics Review*, *5*(1), 23–44.

Wołoszyn, P. (2017a). *Etnografisch onderzoek naar de communicatie tussen de lokale overheden en Poolse arbeidsmigranten in de gemeenten Horst aan de Maas en Peel en Maas*. Amsterdam and Utrecht: Meertens Instituut, Universiteit Utrecht.

Wołoszyn, P. (2017b). *Stageverslag*. Utrecht: Universiteit Utrecht.

Case Study 3

Internal Communication at the University of Aruba

Eric Mijts, Roselinde Supheert,
and Fardau Bamberger

The Case[1]

The University of Aruba (UA) is a small-scale educational institute located in Oranjestad, the capital of Aruba. Approximately 700 students attend higher education at the UA. The University is relatively young: the present University was founded in 1988 and originally occupied one building. The UA has recently gone through a phase of rapid development: personnel quadrupled and the organization now consists of almost 100 full-time employees. This development called for substantial changes, including the introduction of new online communication platforms such as an intranet system for communication among staff (InSite), an application for student record-keeping (Osiris) and a virtual learning environment (EDU20), and the opening of new facilities, including a remote new administrative building. The University now occupies three buildings and is home to four faculties that together offer nine degree programmes and several certificate programmes in the humanities and social sciences Its dense organizational chart illustrates the complexity of the organization (Figure 3.1). One of the UA's most pressing needs is to develop more degree programmes for international and local students in the near future, and to give back to society by doing so. On its website, the UA formulates its mission as: "Serving the Aruban community with knowledge" (University of Aruba, 2016).

Aruba, the smallest of the three ABC islands in the Caribbean, lies just off the coast of Venezuela with a population of 109,028 (CBS Aruba, 2015). The island, which is part of the Kingdom of the Netherlands, has two official languages since 2003, Dutch and Papiamento (Leuverink, 2011). Its inhabitants are generally multilingual and speak, in varying combinations, the dominant languages Papiamento, Dutch, Spanish and English (CBS Aruba, 2010). Dutch is the traditional language of administration, but English is gaining ground in public usage and enjoys high prestige (Bamberger, 2016). Papiamento is spoken in the majority of people's homes (CBS Aruba, 2010).

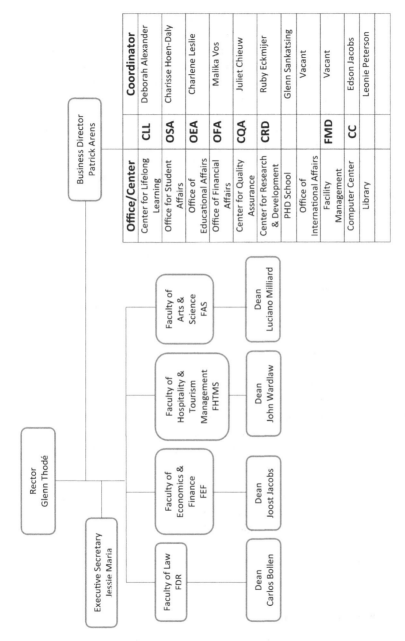

Office/Center		Coordinator
Center for Lifelong Learning	CLL	Deborah Alexander
Office for Student Affairs	OSA	Charisse Hoen-Daly
Office of Educational Affairs	OEA	Charlene Leslie
Office of Financial Affairs	OFA	Malika Vos
Center for Quality Assurance	CQA	Juliet Chieuw
Center for Research & Development	CRD	Ruby Eckmijer
PHD School		Glenn Sankatsing
Office of International Affairs		Vacant
Facility Management	FMD	Vacant
Computer Center	CC	Edson Jacobs
Library		Leonie Peterson

Figure 3.1 Organization Chart of the UA

Although Spanish is quite popular in Aruba, recent research has shown that it mostly enjoys covert prestige among its speakers and that the Arubans' overall image of Spanish immigrants is rather negative (Carroll, 2015).

At the University of Aruba, the languages of instruction are Dutch and English; both languages are used for internal and external administrative communication, but there is a clear preference for English. The UA management indicated that, as a result of its recent growth, it is experiencing a need for change in internal and external communication strategy. Communication problems between organizational clusters, as well as the observation that external communication lacks uniformity and consistency, prompted the UA early in 2016 to appoint an advisory Communication Board (CB) to investigate these issues and formulate a clear communication plan. The small-scale organization of a decade ago allowed for informal, short internal communication lines. In the present, larger organization these informal communication practices may lead to a loss of efficiency and irritation as there is no uniformity in communication practices. The goal of the CB is to streamline internal and external communication of the UA. The CB consists of a selection of lecturers, two management representatives, a journalist, two social media experts, and a communication intern. By means of regular meetings, the current communicational situation at the UA is evaluated, and possible solutions for ongoing issues are discussed. The researcher's role in this process, as an intern at the CB of the UA, was to investigate the current state of *internal communication, to gather input from the work floor, and thus to inventorize bottlenecks.* If the communication problems are solved, the UA will be able to accomplish its goal and mission more efficiently. Considering the previous comments, the following main research question was formulated: What are the bottlenecks of the UA's internal communication strategies and practices and what are its employees' experiences and expectations?

To be able to answer the main research question, the following subquestions were used:

1. What communication channels are used, and what is the employee experience with regard to these channels?
2. To what extent is communication between communicational clusters problematic?
3. In what ways can internal communication at the University of Aruba be improved?

The Research Process

In addition to a preparatory literature review, two methods were used in the present study: interviews and participant observation. Both methods will be described separately. Most data were retrieved from the interviews. Data from participant observation were predominantly used to support statements derived from interview data. The literature will be briefly summarized first.

Literature Review

Communication studies has proved to be relevant for people on an interpersonal level, but it is of great importance at an organizational level as well (Downs & Adrian, 2012). Especially internal communication is among the fastest-expanding fields of research into organizational communication and management studies (Verčič, Verčič, & Sriramesh, 2012). In times of organizational change, improving internal communication appears to be the key to success, as it improves employee engagement and has positive organizational outcomes in general (Proctor & Doukakis, 2003; Karanges, Johnston, Beatson, & Lings, 2015). For organizations aiming to improve internal communication, it is important to know how to assess the communication processes. This can, for instance, be done by means of a communication audit. Communication audits can be implemented in several ways, including interviews, questionnaires, focus groups or panels. The CB described earlier is an example of a panel (Hogendoorn, 2003). Combinations of these methods are recommended (Hogendoorn, 2003) as combining methodologies ensures triangulation, which increases a study's validity (Dörnyei, 2007).

Participant Observation

Three meetings in Dutch of the CB were observed by the intern. Notes, also in Dutch, were made during the meetings and directly after. Meetings began with a short announcement of the topics that were to be discussed. The researcher did not have influence on these topics. The participants that were observed are the members of the CB: lecturers, two management representatives, a journalist and two social media experts. These participants were observed in varying combinations, depending on who was present during each meeting. Table 3.1 lists the observed meetings.

Table 3.1 Overview of Observed Meetings

	Date	Attendees
Meeting 1	29 March 2016	Complete CB
Meeting 2	19 April 2016	Complete CB
Meeting 3	10 May 2016	Journalist
		Social media experts

Interviews

Answers to the present study's research questions were mainly gathered by means of interviews and interview analysis. A number of participants were invited for face-to-face interviews with a semi-structured design. Choosing to conduct interviews with a semi-structured approach will guarantee that all topics of interest are covered in the interview, while at the same time enabling the interviewee to elaborate on topics that the researcher had not foreseen (Dörnyei, 2007).

Participants

The participants for the interviews were chosen after several meetings with the Communication Board of the UA. The business director and a lecturer suggested several participants, after which the intern decided who to approach. As some of the suggested respondents were unavailable, the number of interviewees was raised by means of a snow-ball method. To ensure that different organizational, and hence communicational, clusters were represented in the present study, three categories were distinguished: Management, Education and Support. Table 3.2 shows the participants per category.

Materials

Before the interviews, a topic list was created in preparation. According to Baarda, de Goede, and van der Hulst (2012), topic lists are essential for structured, semi-structured and non-structured interviews, as keeping a topic list in mind guarantees that all relevant topics are covered. The questions were connected to the main topics of research. The interviews began with general questions about the participant's background and position within the organization, after which an inventory of communication channels and participant experience were discussed. Subsequently, the topic changed to participant

Table 3.2 List of Participants

	Category	Abbreviation	Interview language	Country of birth	Gender
1	Management	M1	Dutch	NL	M
2		M2	Dutch	AR	M
3	Education	E1	Dutch	NL	F
4		E2	Dutch	AR	M
5	Support	S1	Dutch	AR	F
6		S2	Dutch	AR	F

experience with these channels and focused on the participant's opinion with regard to improving the channels.

Apart from the topic list, a combined invitation and informed consent document was prepared. The participants received a personal e-mail inviting them for an interview regarding internal communication. The informed consent form was attached to these e-mails and included a summary of the topic. Additionally, the document contained statements regarding privacy. For example, the interviewees were informed of the necessity to record the interviews and of the fact that the information that was shared would be anonymized and treated confidentially.

Procedure

The interviews were mostly held in the participants' offices in May and June 2016. If this was not possible, the researcher arranged an empty office or classroom. In this way, the interviews could be conducted in a quiet environment, which was beneficial to both the conversational quality as well as to the quality of the recordings. The interviews could be held in either English or Dutch, depending on the preference of the interviewee. In the end, all participants chose Dutch. Therefore, all quotations in the present chapter were translated into English by the researcher. The researcher attempted to keep to a set order in which the topics were discussed, but maintained a flexible attitude throughout the conversation. In general, the researcher made use of Baarda et al.'s (2012, p. 33) main structure, in which all interviews start with a short introduction to the topic. Subsequently, an opening question was formulated. All interviews began with the same question, after which the topics from the topic list were discussed one by one. This was the part of the interview that required flexibility, as interviewees occasionally brought up valuable points at unexpected times. Freedom to elaborate on these points was given and the possibility to deviate from the original structure was essential in this case. In the end, the researcher gave her impression of the situation, and the participants were asked whether they thought the researcher's analysis was correct and were given the opportunity to share their insights as well. Finally, the interviewee was thanked and the privacy statements as given in the combined invitation and informed consent document were stressed. The interviewees were able to express their interest in the research outcomes and could ask for the final outcomes if they so desired.

The interviews lasted 30–45 minutes and were recorded with the researcher's mobile phone. Afterwards, the interviews were transcribed using the programme Express Scribe. It must be noted that some parts of the conversation were private or irrelevant and were therefore left out of the transcript. Some statements that were too revealing in terms of privacy had to be erased.

Results

By combining the results from the research methods, it was possible to outline the problems and identify causes. By defining problems, it became easier to find fitting solutions. First the research questions will be answered, after which the advice will be formulated.

1.   What communication channels are used, and what is the employee experience with regard to these channels?

Answers of the interviewees pertaining to the first sub-question were relatively similar, regardless of what group (support staff, education or management) the participants belonged to. The main communication channels that were mentioned were the intranet, e-mail and a variety of social media, though user experience varied. Overall, the mediums that are used at the UA function in the sense that they are operative, though adjustment or regulations are needed. One of the most frequently mentioned mediums of communication was the intranet system InSite. All respondents mentioned InSite, but there was a difference in usage between Management and the other categories. Management not only uses InSite to report their own activities but also to approve requests and reports by their staff. Interviews with supporting staff and educational staff indicated one main problem: even though employees are encouraged by Management and HR to open InSite daily, they do not feel the need to do so, as InSite lacks regular content updates. E-mail was often mentioned as a main means of internal communication. It appears to be used for a variety of messages. It was said that e-mails are used for mass communication (invitations for events, minutes) as well as individual messages. Overall, e-mail was viewed as logically present. Most respondents were positive or neutral about using e-mail, except for one respondent from Management, who stated that there is a proliferation of e-mails. It was striking that UA employees feel they are expected to e-mail in English. Employees used to e-mail in either Dutch, Papiamento or English. However, since the UA has grown, and employs more international staff, the language practice has changed to English to avoid misunderstandings. Surprisingly, perhaps, respondents indicated that, after a short transitional phase, the recent change does not cause any problems. Social media were not used often in internal communication. In general, participants indicated that they do not use social media for internal communication, apart from gathering information from Facebook events occasionally. When asked about the UA's website, respondents stated that they do not use it often for internal communication. On rare occasions it is used to find information concerning specific programmes such as partnerships with other universities.

2. *To what extent is communication between communicational clusters problematic?*

When asked about communication between the clusters, management, educational staff, supporting staff and faculties, interviewees pointed to three central issues. First of all, it appears that most problems originate from an increase in steps that have to be taken to bring information across. This could possibly be related to the recent growth of the UA. This growth has resulted in lines of communication growing longer. Respondents pointed out that this has made communication between all clusters more complex, and that employees are still getting used to new practices, and finding out what to communicate to whom. To fully understand the situation, it is vital to know that many communication practices at the UA are created ad hoc, on a need-driven basis. Respondents also indicated that there is a wish to streamline the organization again, as the quick growth caused the UA's former structure to disintegrate. The increase in student service offices and centres has led to confusion among employees. The opening of a remote administrative location resulted in a dichotomy between employees working in the main building and those who work at the new, remote location. Most respondents stated that, although the new location is necessary, the two buildings are two completely different worlds, which creates a division between employees. Moreover, those who do not work at the main building feel like second-class citizens. The second issue that stands out is that communication between faculties is most problematic, although it seems to be improving. Most respondents stated that the faculties appear to be little islands run according to their own rules. There appears to be some rivalry between faculties, as each of them wants to maintain their own identity. For example, the Faculty of Law is the only faculty with an academic accreditation and the Faculty of Hospitality and Tourism Management Studies is the only faculty that follows the US education system in the sense that grading and credits differ from the European system, as used by the other faculties. Third, most respondents expressed a preference for informal over formal communication. All respondents mentioned that they were used to communicating informally with one another in the hallways. This was perceived as more fruitful than hearing information through formal channels.

3. *In what ways can internal communication at the UA be improved?*

Even though not all respondents could name one major cause for problems at the UA, they all had suggestions for improvement. Suggestions for adjustments and improvements can generally be divided in two categories. On the one hand, respondents offered practical, small-scaled solutions. On the other hand, major, substantial solutions were proposed. The need for InSite updates was often mentioned. Updates would encourage employees to open InSite daily. Moreover, there is a general desire to know when new staff arrives, and when staff members leave. Furthermore, InSite is felt to be not flexible. For instance, the system does not include an option to change earlier posts. The respondents pointed to Human Resources, who own the tool, to add more information regarding incoming and outgoing staff and fix InSite's inflexibilities. Several respondents also mentioned the abundance of meetings between clusters that are held. It was also said that the meetings that are held are not always effective; people discuss many irrelevant, personal issues during meetings. Several respondents mentioned that there was a plan to make a public bulletin after each meeting, in addition to private minutes, to inform the other clusters of what had been discussed. These plans were never executed. Some respondents also thought it might be helpful to merge all faculties into one.

Consultancy and Acceptance

All in all, the UA's difficulties in internal communication are caused by an increase of employees and students. An extra location was opened to meet the need for more space, but the physical and mental distance between the two locations creates a gap between employees. On top of that, the additional layers between communication clusters resulted in information being lost and projects delayed. Furthermore, lines of communication grew longer. Based on the research, the following points, mentioned by the respondents, are important in the UA's transformation to a larger, professional organization:

- To reduce the dichotomy between the two locations, it is important to focus on both long-term solutions, such as finding a building closer to the central one, as well as on an equal distribution of events over both buildings.
- To meet the demands for straightforward communication, student service offices and centres need to be streamlined to keep employees from working on the same task without being aware of this.
- Merging all faculties into one might be useful, but this should not be a priority, as not all faculties are ready for the change.
- InSite should become a more flexible, pro-active platform that offers more information regarding staff members.

In addition to the advice as formulated by the respondents, the following points were formulated by the researcher as additional advice:

- Where the UA could first depend on informal communication, the organization now needs to adapt to the more formal approach to communication a larger organization calls for.
- Additionally, information sessions regarding updates on the expansion of facilities and buildings could be organized. This would show employees that management is aware of the issue and is actively attempting to solve it.
- InSite could be used as an interactive platform where staff can reflect on changes and communication problems. Questionnaires or polls could be used to gather additional information in this respect.

The preceding advice was presented to the business director of the UA in a final meeting. He indicated that some of these points are on the UA's agenda already. For example, the UA is currently negotiating the use of a building nearby.

Final Reflection

Contrary to the researcher's original expectations, the problems seem to have originated from the growth of the organization rather than from the multicultural society of which it is a part. For instance, multilingual communication, or the change to writing all e-mails in English, does not appear to have had negative consequences for internal communication at the UA. It is the style of communication (formal versus informal) rather than the choice of language that causes problems. The researcher initially focused on finding miscommunication between cultures in the more traditional sense of the word, but discovered that intercultural differences between organizations (such as small organizations versus large organizations) should be taken into account as well.

Note

1 This chapter is based on applied research conducted by Fardau Bamberger in the context of her research internship with the University of Aruba (April–July 2016, supervised by Eric Mijts and Roselinde Supheert) and the resulting internship report.

References

Baarda, B., de Goede, M., & van der Hulst, M. (2012). *Basisboek Interviewen: Handleiding voor het voorbereiden en afnemen van interviews*. Groningen and Houten: Noordhoff Uitgevers.

44   *Eric Mijts et al.*

Bamberger, F. (2016). *The role of English in Aruba's linguistic landscape: Representation of Aruba's four dominant languages in written form in the public sphere* (Master's thesis). Retrieved from https://studenttheses.library.uu.nl/search. php?language=en

Carroll, K. S. (2015). Language maintenance in the Caribbean: Examining perceptions of threat in Aruba and Puerto Rico. *Language Problems & Language Planning, 39*(2), 115–135. doi:10.1075/lplp.39.2.01car

CBS Aruba. (2010). Population by language most spoken in the household by age and sex. *Censo 2010 Aruba*. Retrieved from www.censo2010.aw/index.php

CBS Aruba. (2015, 2nd quarter). Population figures CBS versus DBSB: Why the discrepancy. *Quarterly Demographic Bulletin*. Retrieved from http://cbs.aw/wp/ wp-content/uploads/2016/04/QDB0615.pdf

Dörnyei, Z. (2007). *Research methods in applied linguistics*. Oxford: Oxford University Press.

Downs, C., & Adrian, A. (2012). *Assessing organizational communication: Strategic communication audits*. New York: Guilford Press.

Hogendoorn, M. (2003). *Communicatieonderzoek*. Bussum: Uitgeverij Coutinho.

Karanges, E., Johnston, K., Beatson, A., & Lings, I. (2015). The influence of internal communication on employee engagement: A pilot study. *Public Relations Review, 41*(1), 129–131.

Leuverink, K. (2011). *Un Idioma Strano: Een Macamba over Nederlands als vreemde taal in Aruba* (Master's thesis). University of Amsterdam, Amsterdam. Retrieved from http://dare.uva.nl/document/444134

Proctor, T., & Doukakis, I. (2003). Change management: The role of internal communication and employee development. *Corporate Communications: An International Journal, 8*(4), 268–277.

University of Aruba. (2016). *About the university of Aruba*. University of Aruba. Retrieved from www.ua.aw/about-the-ua/

Verčič, A., Verčič, D., & Sriramesh, K. (2012). Internal communication: Definition, parameters, and the future. *Public Relations Review, 38*(2), 223–230.

Case Study 4

Lingua Receptiva at the Directorate-General for Translation (DGT) of the European Commission

Jan D. ten Thije

The Case

"Unity in diversity" is the motto of the European Community. In the expansion of the European Union in 2004, 2007 and 2013 to a total of 24 countries, this basic principle poses a challenge to the policy of multilingualism. According to the language policy agreed upon in 1959 by the six countries that founded the EEC, all national standard languages are equal. Every European citizen must be able to communicate with the European Commission in the national language or languages of their country. This means that all official documents have to be available in every standard language of all the member states. With new countries joining the European Union a greater appeal is made to the Directorate-General for Translation. With the six member states in 1959 translation between the four standard languages (French, German, Italian and Dutch) was quite feasible. However, with 24 languages it is a costly affair which also leads to organizational problems since the number of translators of the so-called small languages is limited. Within the Directorate-General for Translation, thought has been given to cost reduction and ways to optimise and efficiently organize the translation process between 24 languages.

In this context, in 2011 the Unit of Multilingualism of the Directorate-General for Translation was tasked to write a memo on the possible role of Intercomprehension in the translation process. Intercomprehension is a form of multilingual communication in which people use different languages, but can still understand each other on account of their receptive competencies in the language of the other. Various terms for this form of multilingual communication can be found in the literature (Backus et al., 2013; ten Thije, 2018). The concept of *Intercomprehension* is used when the languages involved derive from the same language family. French and Spanish, for instance, belong to the Romance language family, and in the same way Dutch and German belong to the Germanic language family. The notion of *Receptive Multilingualism* is used to refer to multilingual communication in which members use their language and understand each other even if they speak languages that do not belong to the same language families. For instance, users of the French language can understand German as well, if they have acquired and developed sufficient receptive competencies in German. Rehbein, ten Thije, and Verschik (2012) have introduced a third notion that highlights another aspect of multilingual communication. The notion *lingua receptiva* (the Dutch term is *luistertaal*) refers to multilingual interaction in which participants do not use their L1 but another language receptively – an L2 or a lingua franca – to understand other participants. The quintessence behind all these concepts is that people use different languages and can understand each other on the basis of the receptive knowledge of the language of the other.

At a conference in 2011 the author got into a conversation with an employee of the Multilingualism Unit and subsequently received an invitation to come to Brussels to discuss the concept of Intercomprehension. His expertise is mainly in oral multilingual communication, among other things because of his supervision of research into receptive multilingualism in the Dutch-German border region (Beerkens, 2010). He also contributed to a report on Intercomprehension published in 2012 (EU Commission, 2012). This report includes an elaborate proposal by Grin, a Swiss language economist, aiming to simplify the translation process at the Directorate-General for Translation. It proposes dividing the 24 European Union languages into 10 language groups within which mutual intelligibility could be possible. This European Union report is the point of departure of this case (ibid.).

After the publication of the report, the author and the Directorate-General for Translation remained in contact. The aim of the cooperation was to come to an advice with regard to the role oral and written receptive multilingualism could play in the realisation of more efficient communication at the DGT and the European Commission in general. As a first result three DGT professionals were willing to cooperate in making a video documentary that was produced by honours students of Utrecht University in 2012.[1] In the video documentary attention is paid to Lingua Receptiva in diverse settings: the Euregio between Münster and Enschede, a Dutch-German bilingual family, dialect-speaking families in Limburg and the European parliament and the Directorate-General for Translation in Brussels. The video documentary seemed to bode well for a successful cooperation between Utrecht University and the Directorate-General for Translation. In practice, however, this would prove to be rather complex.

The Research Process

Two researchers – students of the Master's programme in Intercultural Communication in Utrecht – were prepared to do research on Intercomprehension at the Directorate-General for Translation. The research consisted of a series of interviews with Directorate-General for Translation professionals on their attitude and experiences with Intercomprehension in the Directorate-General for Translation workplace. Special attention was paid to the role that Intercomprehension plays or could play in the many translations the Directorate-General for Translation has to produce daily. The assumption was that Intercomprehension could reduce costs.

A first major obstacle turned out to be receiving the formal approval to execute this research within the hierarchy of the Directorate-General for Translation, which approval was to be obtained by the Multilingualism Unit from the board of directors and the responsible Member of the European Commission. The approval took two months, which is not unusual within the strongly hierarchically organized European Commission. In the meantime, the students involved struggled with the planning of their studies due to the time available for writing their theses. Meanwhile they executed various other tasks within the Lingua Receptiva project, like the creation of a *Wikipedia* page on Lingua Receptiva and the development of a website on lingua receptiva.[2]

Once the approval was granted, everything happened quickly. The Directorate-General for Translation contact person had arranged 15 conversations with as many professionals with different positions at different Directorate-General for Translation units. These professionals were all chosen by the Directorate-General for Translation employee, which makes it hard to decide to what extent the respondents were a representative reflection of the Directorate-General for Translation personnel. The students collected the data in two days. The semi-structured interviews were well prepared. A questionnaire was ready with clusters of questions about personal details, attitudes towards the use of Intercomprehension in different contexts and (receptive) linguistic capacities in different languages. After analysis, the results were incorporated in two Master's theses, one focusing on written language use and containing the description of the translation process within the Directorate-General for Translation (Van Klaveren, 2013), and the other focusing on oral language use within the Directorate-General for Translation and the role Intercomprehension/Lingua Receptiva plays in this, or could play (De Vries, 2013).

The results of the research can be summarised as follows. The Directorate-General for Translation turned out to be a specific communicative setting with highly language-proficient professionals, which might have influenced the results. The vast majority of Directorate-General for Translation employees ($n = 15$) were familiar with Intercomprehension and used it, both in oral and written communication. All possible language combinations were used by applying Intercomprehension. For instance, colleagues were talking French and English to each other, or German and Dutch, or Spanish and

Portuguese. Factors such as personal relationships, linguistic background, linguistic competencies, location and subject determined the use of Intercomprehension. Intercomprehension was mostly used in informal situations and with acquaintances. In formal situations and communication with strangers, a lingua franca (e.g. English) was used more often. The majority considered Intercomprehension an efficient way of communication; this multilingual mode gives you many opportunities to explain your intents or plans several times. Making jokes is also easier in your L1. Talking your L1 especially for interaction within a small group is an efficient multilingual mode. In case the size of the group increases a lingua franca becomes more feasible. The respondents were positive about the possibility to participate in an Intercomprehension training, both language-specific and general. This will be described below in some more detail. With regard to the relevance of Intercomprehension for the translation process, the employees thought it might increase the efficiency of the translation process. However, risks relating to quality control, efficiency and political sensitivities should be considered as well. These risks could be neutralised by only using Intercomprehension for internal documents. All respondents thought Intercomprehension should be the subject of more research since they acknowledge its potential.

Consultancy and Acceptance

The research resulted in advice to the board of directors of the Directorate-General for Translation (Van Klaveren, ten Thije, & De Vries, 2013). Besides the most important results of the analysis, the advice contains three recommendations. The recommendations are:

* Use the term *Lingua Receptiva* instead of *Intercomprehension*, because the former term has a broader definition and therefore offers a more successful implementation within the Directorate-General for Translation;
* Organize an awareness training on the potential of Lingua Receptiva for efficient communication within the Directorate-General for Translation;
* Organize a large-scale investigation to map the efficiency of translating by means of Lingua Receptiva.

The advice was presented in Brussels within the Directorate-General for Translation to the employees of the department concerned and offered to the board of directors of the Directorate-General for Translation. An official written reaction of the director of Directorate-General for Translation to the advice was never received.

Looking back, it can be concluded there may be a specific reason for the Directorate-General for Translation's lack of response. This reason has to do with the change in language policy within the Directorate-General for Translation. It turns out that the recommendations of Grin, proposed in the publication of 2012, will not be implemented either. There is apparent resistance within the Directorate-General for Translation against the proposal to divide the translation process and classify the translations in 10 language groups. The Directorate-General for Translation chose another model of translation. Finances certainly play a role in this. In short, all documents are first translated into English or written directly in English. Subsequently, the documents are translated into the 24 standard languages of the European Union. Texts are not translated anymore between all languages of the European Union, but only from and to English. The fact that not enough translators are available for all language combinations also plays a role in this. The Directorate-General for Translation is being reorganized, and the English unit expanded substantially. The other 23 units are all organized in such a way that translations are only made from English into language X. In this model, there seems no room for Intercomprehension. The advice of Utrecht University ended up at the bottom of a big pile of paper somewhere in European Union offices.

The Research Process Continued

Three years later in November 2016 the author unexpectedly received an invitation from our contact person at the Directorate-General for Translation to participate in the first broadcast of Radio Linguistika. This is a podcast that the Directorate-General for Translation sets up for internal information and communication among the DGT employees in Brussels and Luxembourg. The first broadcast was devoted entirely to Intercomprehension. Not only was there a renewed interest in the Utrecht University advice on Intercomprehension given earlier, attention was also paid to the Directorate-General for Translation's pilot in the Spanish and Portuguese unit. In this pilot, efficient cooperation was attempted in the translation of an English text into Spanish or Portuguese. This meant that of four English texts, two are translated into Portuguese and the other two into Spanish. The two Portuguese texts were subsequently translated into Spanish and the two Spanish texts into Portuguese. In this translation process use was made of linguistic closeness, which bears close resemblance to the use of Intercomprehension. The question that needed to be answered by the pilot was if this form of Intercomprehension is efficient and if it guarantees the intended quality of translation. This pilot exemplifies that Intercomprehension is relevant from two perspectives. In fact

Intercomprehension may improve the multilingual communication in the workplace and could support the quality control of the translation process.

The broadcast brought the cooperation between Brussels and Utrecht to life again and there also appeared to be an interest in an awareness training. Two researchers – students of the Master's programme in Intercultural Communication – conducted follow-up research into the use of Intercomprehension and developed an awareness training (Postma, 2017). In addition to the Directorate-General for Translation, the research also focused on the Directorate-General for Education and Culture (DGEAC) (Wery, 2017). By means of semi-structured interviews it was explored how employees experience and value the use of Intercomprehension and which are the factors that determine the success of Intercomprehension usage. This research confirms the results of previous research (Van Klaveren, 2013; De Vries, 2013). A majority of the respondents (8 out of 13) appeared to be familiar with the phenomenon of Intercomprehension and make use of it in some, mainly informal, situations. They have a positive attitude towards Intercomprehension, but in formal communication English as lingua franca still appears to play a dominant role. The interviews revealed that in the light of Brexit the French language is becoming more important. Colleagues of the Directorate-General for Translation still showed an interest in the application of Intercomprehension in their translation work but, in comparison to the previous research in 2013, little progress appeared to have been made in this field.

In June 2017 within the Directorate-General for Translation two awareness trainings, of four hours each, were offered. The training in Luxembourg had 10 participants and in Brussels 16 participants. These participants did not participate in the research mentioned before. The most important aims of the training were:

- To list and reflect upon practices of Intercomprehension which are already being used in translation work.
- To explore the idea of Intercomprehension being beneficial to the internal communication within this Directorate.
- To raise awareness of the advantages and limitations of Intercomprehension as a multilingual mode within the framework of the Language Policy of the European Commission.
- To stimulate the use of the multilingual competencies of employees.

Besides a theoretical introduction on Intercomprehension the training consisted of a practical exercise in which the participants had to execute two similar tasks in couples, one task in English as lingua franca and the other using Intercomprehension. The couples were formed on the basis of language skills (passive and active) of the Directorate-General for Translation employees, and the couples were instructed beforehand which languages they should use for the second task. Some couples were to use Intercomprehension within one language family (e.g. Spanish-Italian) and in other cases, different language families were combined (e.g. Chinese-French). The discussion with the participants at the end of the training gave insight into which interaction strategies might foster the success of Intercomprehension. In addition, it became clear that understanding could be gained asymmetrically by means of Intercomprehension, because the passive knowledge of the language of the other can differ notably among the members of a couple. This does not mean that mutual intelligibility is impossible, but that the conversational partners have to adjust their strategies for it to work.

Finally, the relevance of Intercomprehension for the translation process within the DGT was discussed. The participants signalled the current daily practices of Intercomprehension and the following potential applications at the Directorate-General for Translation:

- The employees formulated suggestions regarding the current translation model, in which all texts have to be translated from English. This sometimes leads to translators having to work with badly formulated English texts, which, in turn, leads to extra work because of extra checks. The previously mentioned Directorate-General for Translation pilot with the Spanish/Portuguese department was assessed positively. More reflection on the translation procedure is needed in order to increase the efficiency of the Directorate-General for Translation (Backus et al., 2013).
- When translating a text from English into another language, it is profitable to compare the results with the translations of the same text within the same language family. This contributes to the overall quality of the translations.
- With respect to terminology in a specific domain (e.g. agriculture) participants see the advantage of regular contact and exchange with colleagues within and across language boundaries in order to create a stable and adequate terminology for all 24 European languages.
- Some colleagues participating in the training already experience Intercomprehension in daily internal communication at the Directorate-General for Translation. Others were convinced, by this training, of the potential of Intercomprehension for their daily work.
- In order to increase their translation potential, many employees of Directorate-General for Translation follow language courses at the DGT. It appears to them that if their multilingual repertoire is taken as a starting point, other languages can be learned more efficiently. In fact, Intercomprehension/Lingua Receptiva can also be used as a didactic strategy.

A report of the outcomes of the training was sent to the Directorate-General for Translation, as well as an offer to repeat the training, so as to stimulate the discussion on an efficient translation policy.

Final Reflection

A lesson to be learned from this case study is that cooperation and consultancy of large institutions like the European Commission requires a great deal of patience and perseverance. Contacts during the awareness training indicated that translators might be open to new approaches, including Lingua Receptiva, even if these did not turn out to be much more efficient. They would appreciate more variety in their translations. Their work is now very much determined by translating what they call "Pidgin English originals." However, it is the hierarchy of the Directorates that blocks these attempts. Managers fear that these innovations disturb the efficiency of translating all European languages in which process English has a central position. The efficiency is increased and costs are reduced by replacing translators with freelancers and machine translations. In consequence, according to the translators, the role of English seems to be a sort of dogma which is never openly admitted. The Directorate-General for Translation formally promotes multilingualism (e.g. unity in diversity), though the gap between theory and practice widens. It is very difficult to account for this contradiction. The awareness training was highly appreciated by the translators. It is hoped we will be allowed to offer a sequel within the regular training offered by the HR department of Directorate-General for Translation.

Notes

1. This Dutch video documentary with English subtitles has been last viewed on 31 July 2017 on https://youtu.be/TU5k8WEBuD0.
2. The *Wikipedia* page can be visited at https://nl.wikipedia.org/wiki/Lingua_receptiva and the website on lingua receptiva (i.e. luistertaal) at www.luistertaal.nl.

References

Backus, A., Gorter, D., Knapp, K., Schjerve-Rindler, R., Swanenberg, J., ten Thije, J. D., & Vetter, E. (2013). Inclusive multilingualism: Concept, modes and implications. *European Journal for Applied Linguistics*, *1*(2), 179–215.

Beerkens, R. (2010). *Receptive multilingualism as a language mode in the Dutch-German border area*. Münster: Waxmann Verlag.

De Vries, J. (2013). *Lingua receptiva in de schriftelijke communicatie van de Europese Commissie. Een onderzoek naar de praktijk en potentie van lingua receptiva voor een efficiënter vertaalproces binnen het directoraat-generaal Vertaling voor de*

Europese Commissie (Unpublished master's thesis). Utrecht University, Utrecht, The Netherlands.

European Commission. (2012). *Studies on multilingualism and translation: Intercomprehension.* Luxembourg: Publications Office of the European Union.

Postma, H. (2017). *Het potentieel van lingua receptiva in de Europese Commissie. Een onderzoek naar de implementatie van 'lingua receptiva' binnen het Directoraat-generaal Vertaling van de Europese Commissie* (Unpublished master's thesis). Utrecht University, Utrecht, The Netherlands.

Rehbein, J., ten Thije, J. D., & Verschik, A. (2012). Lingua receptiva (LaRa) – remarks on the quintessence of receptive multilingualism. *International Journal of Bilingualism, 16*(3), 248–264.

ten Thije, J. D. (2018). Receptive multilingualism. In D. Singleton & L. Aronin (Eds.), *Twelve lectures on multilingualism* (pp. 327–362). Bristol and Blue Ridge Summit: Multilingual Matters.

Van Klaveren, S. (2013). *Lingua receptiva in mondelinge communicatie. Een onderzoek naar de praktijk van lingua receptiva voor een efficiëntere communicatie binnen het Directoraat-Generaal Vertaling van de Europese Commissie* (Unpublished master's thesis). Utrecht University, Utrecht, The Netherlands.

Van Klaveren, S., ten Thije, J. D., & De Vries, J. (2013). *Practices and potentials of intercomprehension: Research into the efficiency of intercomprehension with regard to the workflow at the directorate-general for translation of the European commission.* Utrecht: Utrecht University.

Wery, A. (2017). *The use and potential of lingua receptiva at the European commission: An explorative research on the internal communication and translation processes at DGT and DGEAC* (Unpublished master's thesis). Utrecht University, Utrecht, The Netherlands.

Part II
Commercial Organizations

Case Study 5
Acquisition Within One Country
How Two Organizational Cultures
Come Together

Roos Beerkens

The Case

The client here concerns a large retail organization in the Netherlands. For reasons of confidentiality, the client will remain anonymous. The client had taken over another large retail organization in the Netherlands. Although both organizations have the same core business, they could not be more different, especially concerning their history and organizational culture.[1] The take-over had to be successful, which means that the result had to be a successful integration of the two organizations. As a communication consultant working for a communication consultancy firm, I was asked to contribute to this goal; to smooth the integration process and make sure it resulted in one integrated organization, using a strategy that fit the acquiring organization. The question focused on internal communication within the organization.[2]

The client's question was obviously inspired by fear of failure of the acquisition. In cross-border mergers and acquisitions, roughly one in two turn out to be unsuccessful (Barmeyer & Mayrhofer, 2008). The most frequently mentioned causes are cultural differences and communicative misunderstandings. In this case, the acquired organization was within the same country. However, it is from a different part of the Netherlands and has a different history; one organization being a family-owned company and the other being led by investors. The management team of the acquiring organization was aware of the fact that these differences had resulted in very different organizational cultures, which could lead to communicative misunderstandings that would be a threat to a successful acquisition. Therefore, the management team decided to set up a project team to guide the integration process with the following experts: an integration manager, a project team leader, an IT specialist, a financial specialist, an HR consultant and myself as communication consultant. The project team was a mix of employees from both organizations and two external consultants.

The acquiring organization had shown strong economic growth in a short period of time, indicating that its strategy was strong enough to gain a large share of the market. Its management team, consisting of several family members and others, was therefore convinced that the strategy should remain as it was. They were not only convinced that the strategy was the better one, they were also convinced that the organizational culture that has evolved over time is a strong asset. Their employees feel they are part of the family, and they feel individually proud because of the rapid growth of the firm. This has engendered a strong sense of community in the organization. The acquired organization, on the other hand, was in a different position. The organization had been sold to investors several times and the current management team was happy to be taken over by one of the strongest players on the market. The management team had seen many managers depart over the years, leading to a lack of clear leadership for all employees. Those that stayed did, however, feel proud of the fact that the brand was still alive and were convinced that their, more corporate, way of working was effective.

The integration team cooperated closely because of the many challenges, among others the re-branding of 300 shops, cutting about 25% of the head office employees, integration of IT systems, reorganization of the logistics planning and locations. Not only the shops would get a make-over, the employees working there would have to start working for a different brand and get used to a new organization, including different systems, products, and of course, a different organizational culture. After a few useful meetings with the integration manager it became clear that every aspect of the integration process included two potentially crucial aspects: communication and culture. Because the process was so complex and the integration was planned over a period of three years, it was agreed that all integration project team members would work full-time on the project, dividing time between the locations of the two organizations. It was my task as a communication consultant to make a communication plan that fully aligned with the strategic integration plan and implement the communication plan for the first year and a half. Hence, the question asked concerns the research process, the advice (communication plan) and the implementation of the advice. The reason for combining these is that reality shows integration processes to be unpredictable and 'change requires change'. As predicted, the plan presented and discussed in the beginning was updated regularly during the one and a half years.

The Research Process

To decide on the most suitable plan for communication about the integration process, an iterative and pragmatic approach was chosen. Iterative means that I shuttled between the research phase and implementation during the project. This was necessary because the situation had 'change' written all over it; two organizations had to integrate, which means that everything and everyone was going through change. Accordingly, the communication plan also needed to be adjusted from time to time. Careful monitoring was crucial for the process. The approach had to be pragmatic, because of time pressure; I had to deliver the communication plan fast (within two months), because the acquisition had already been announced and rumours had started about possible consequences of the integration. The so-called process of sense-making (Weick, 1995) had already started: employees needed to give meaning to the things that were going on. It is crucial for an organization going through change that management takes the lead in this process of sense-making. Therefore, internal communication to and with employees was urgently needed.

The first phase took about eight weeks, in which several research methods were combined:

1. *Ethnographic observation*: Because I was working at locations of the two organizations five days a week, I was able to observe the behaviour of people within the organizations in their own habitat. This is a good method to get insight into the organizational cultures. Besides, I was able to analyse the formal and informal communicative structures in both organizations, experiencing communication just as employees from the acquired organization would experience communication from the acquiring organization.

2. *Interviews with management team members*: Several interviews were performed with management members from both organizations. The aim of the interviews was to find out: 1) what the goals of the integration process were for each of the management members, and 2) where they saw bumps in the road or issues that needed to be tackled or could be problematic for the integration process. The analysis of these interviews was useful, because it gave insight in the two organizational cultures as well as which issues were relevant to address in communication with employees.

3. *Interviews with employees from different departments and levels in both organizations*: Talking to employees from different departments and levels in both organizations revealed a different aspect of the integration process, namely the emotional aspect. Many employees knew that in both organizations a certain number of employees would be laid off. This led to great uncertainty and fear among most teams. On top of that, it was very unclear what would happen to the acquired organization's brand. Employees from the acquired organization were afraid and angry about the lack of clarity on this topic, whereas employees from the acquiring organization were surprised that the brand was an issue at all, since they were so convinced their own brand and strategy were much stronger. Information like this is something that comes to the surface when talking

to people, and showing an interest in what worries them. One of the other goals of these interviews was to find out which employees could be strategically used as 'communication network members', or to put it more simply: find out who were the eyes and ears of the organization. Usually, these are people who have been working at an organization for a longer period of time, and are engaged and therefore willing to share information with the project team and discuss matters with employees.

4. *Analysis of statistics from the intranet*: Both organizations had already informed their employees about the acquisition via the intranet messaging. Statistics showed how often these messages were opened and gave insight into the integration topics employees thought most interesting. Ongoing measuring and monitoring was done throughout the integration process.

After the first phase of gathering and analysing information I had a clear picture of the state of affairs in both organizations. I discussed all results with the integration team and made the first version of the communication plan. I did this in the form of a PowerPoint presentation with visuals that were explained in speaker notes underneath each slide. This format was chosen because it was a commonly used format in both organizations. This way, it was also easier to discuss the plan with others. Especially the management team members, who were important stakeholders in this case, did not have time to read a full report and were more comfortable dealing with Power-Point presentations.

Consultancy and Acceptance

As in all change management research processes (e.g. Barmeyer & Mayrhofer, 2008), conducting interviews and being there as a researcher/consultant turned out to be interventions already. Interviewing employees and management team members was also the start of the adoption of the communication plan. What is crucial in this case is that the entire integration process was a process of acceptation. Everybody, including management team members, had to get used to the fact that two organizational cultures had to become one. It was part of my job to get people to accommodate to this process and accept change. However, the first step was to get the management team members to approve and believe in the communication plan, a strategy aimed at acceptance and realisation of the integration process by them and all employees in both organizations. This chapter focuses on the core ideas of the advice, followed by strategies used to engage the main communication stakeholders.

The communication plan could only be successful if it fit the goals of the integration process, goals that all members and all sub-project teams working on the integration topic would subscribe to. These goals were unclear at the time I joined the team. The first intervention was to organize meetings that would lead to clear goals of the integration, so that all project members could make sure their plans would fit one shared strategy. After two meetings, the goals that the management team members and the integration project team agreed upon were clear. The second step was to define communication goals to help achieve the three main goals. These were defined as follows: 1) create a support base among all managers and employees for all changes going on, 2) give clarity on factual changes, 3) stimulate behaviour and an organizational culture that match the changes (with respect for the fact that people need time to change). The metaphor of a zipper (see Figure 5.1) was used to illustrate the integration process; step by step we had to make sure that two organizations became one.

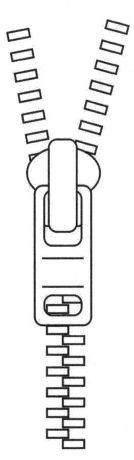

Figure 5.1 The Zipper Metaphor Used to Illustrate the Integration Process

Core of the Communication Plan

The translation of these three goals led to three main pillars on which the communication plan was built:

1. *Formal exchange of information*: Before people can accept change and become engaged, it is important to provide them with enough information, enabling them to understand the impact of the integration process and the choices that have to be made. Information was provided via several key communicative players in the organization (not only management team members, but also team leaders, communication network employees and employees with specific expertise), via several communicative means (intranet, newsletters, mailings, workshops, lunch meetings etc.), and via feedback gathered throughout the organization which provided input for lunch meetings and newsletters, for example.
2. *Facilitating communication for employees involved*: During the integration process, about 20% of all employees were in some way involved in projects that contributed to integrating the two organizations. The communication of these people was facilitated; they were supported in setting up meeting structures for projects, document sharing systems, organizing feedback loops and the means of communication mentioned under #1 gave them access to the rest of the information.
3. *Specific communication with impact:* The entire integration process took about three years. During that period, there were quite a few milestones that required specific attention and communication advice. Three main milestones which had great impact were the integration of separate departments, the resignation process led by HR and the re-branding of the shops. For each project, separate communication plans were made, making sure the main stakeholders could work with the plans. For example, for the integration of separate departments casual lunch meetings were organized where employees from both organizations could meet and were stimulated to discuss what they thought was good or bad about the other organization. This helped people to get to know the 'others' and speak their mind. For one of the other major milestones – the redundancies – a manual and workshop for team leaders was organized to prepare them for conversations with employees who were being made redundant and for providing after-care for these employees.

For these three topics and the sub-topics, two main basic premises were formulated:

a. Make sure all written and spoken messages from communications and the main communicative players are aligned; speak with one voice.

b. The main task from communications is not to send information, but to facilitate the main communicative players and stakeholders in their communicative tasks.

The preceding represents the core of the communication plan. The three main pillars lead to sub-topics and those lead to concrete actions, of which some are mentioned as examples. It is beyond the scope of this chapter to discuss all. In 18 months, much was done. The pillars remained the same throughout the process, but the focus changed according to the strategic shifts the acquiring organization had to make over time. Flexibility was key in the entire process.

Adoption

Before the research could be conducted, the planning for the research process had to be approved by the integration manager and the management team. Examples from similar case studies helped to convince the most important stakeholders to invest in the research process. In addition, all management team members were aware of the fact that in order to make a proper communication plan, it was necessary to get to know both organizational cultures.

The second step was to convince several stakeholders of the communication plan. These stakeholders were the integration team, the management team and the communication teams of both organizations. This was already done during the research process; as mentioned previously, the interviews with management team members were seen as an intervention in itself. From both communication teams, one employee was invited for an interview. In addition, during the research process (of about eight weeks), weekly updates were presented to the integration team and the management team, and I joined bi-weekly communication team meetings where I also gave updates. Here I also asked for input, for example, who to approach for interviews and what to focus on when observing. Hence, the research process became a shared process.

A third step towards adoption of the communication plan was to discuss the communicative responsibility of the management team members and mention it as one of the important assets in the communication plan. It was agreed that the communication consultant should not be the voice of the management team, but that they should use their own voice, and that they would be fully facilitated in doing that in an aligned and professional way. So, adopting the communication plan meant acknowledging their own communicative responsibility and taking it seriously. Because they had been fully involved in the research process from the beginning, this made perfect sense to them.

Implementation

The implementation of the communication plan started immediately after the plan was approved. There was a great need for information, and many communicative players needed to be facilitated in their communicative tasks. Because I was also asked to implement the communication plan, I could monitor all communication activities easily, and adjust the plan when necessary. This turned out to be useful.

The communication team members of both organizations helped me implement the communication plan. Some tasks could be seen as part of the regular communication activities, which lead to alignment with regular means of communication messages. Other tasks were done by me, but I always kept the teams updated. It soon emerged that it was very important to be clear about who had which responsibilities in order to prevent flaws in the implementation of the plan.

The plan turned out to be successful; when employees received more information and could discuss the information with peers and managers in the organization, they felt heard. In addition, it turned out that employees appreciated the fact that the management team and integration team acknowledged the differences between the organizational cultures and the emotions that came with the acquisition. Listening to people, giving them a voice, getting feedback and questions, and facilitating everyone in their communicative responsibilities were key aspects of the communication plan and very much appreciated. After one and a half years I left the organization, and made sure the communication team was trained to take over the role I had had. By that time, the sentiment in the organization had changed and a new organizational culture was developing. Sharing all this information, and having discussions and meetings, employees had tried to distill the best of both organizations and integrate this in the new one.

Final Reflection

Because the plan was so all-embracing it was sometimes hard to decide which projects or activities to prioritize. The communication plan initially followed the overall integration project plan, but of course, not everything in the process went exactly according to plan. At those times it was important to discuss priorities with the integration manager, and if necessary, with the management team. Sometimes, reality kicked in and daily business turned out to be more important than the integration project. It was important to acknowledge then that the focus was partly gone for the time being, instead of pushing people too much.

During the process all four research methods were regularly repeated. Observation was an ongoing process, although it must be noted that once I worked longer for the organization, observing as a neutral researcher became harder. This is not surprising, since I became a member of the 'family' myself. As a member of the integration team I regularly had to discuss matters with management team members, including the family members. Because I was also responsible for the implementation of the communication plan, I felt very much engaged in the process and therefore lost the neutral perspective of an outsider. To make sure the communication plan was still on track, I asked one of my senior colleagues from the consultancy firm to give feedback and in that way, I could still involve the outsider perspective.

The most important activity in this consultancy job was to talk to the most important stakeholders; to listen to what they had to say at all times during the process was key. At the same time flexibility was needed; the market was growing and changing and therefore the integration process had to follow those changes. A lack of flexibility would have made the communication plan useless.

Notes

1. For literature on organizational culture see Schein, E. (1984). Coming to a new awareness of organizational culture. *Sloan Management Review*, *25*(2), 3–16.
2. Internal communication has many definitions. Working for the communication consultancy firm I followed a broad definition of IC, namely everything that one can hear, see or read within an organization (see Van Ravenstein & Kok, 2014).

References

Barmeyer, C., & Mayrhofer, U. (2008). The contribution of intercultural management to the success of mergers and acquisitions: An analysis of the EADS group. *International Business Review*, *17*(1), 28–38.

Schein, E. (1984). Coming to a new awareness of organizational culture. *Sloan Management Review*, *25*(2), 3–16.

Van Ravenstein, I., & Kok, G. (2014). IC in 3D. In *Interne communicatie in een breed organisatieperspectief* (2nd ed.). Amsterdam: Adfo Groep.

Weick, K. E. (1995). *Sensemaking in organizations*. Newbury Park, CA: Sage.

Case Study 6

Enhancing Team Effectiveness for an Executive Team in Saudi Arabia

*Jürgen Hell, Jules Bolhuis, and
Roselinde Supheert*

The Case

The client is a market-leading pharmacy retailer, operating more than 1,000 stores throughout the Kingdom of Saudi Arabia. As in most large enterprises in Saudi Arabia, the board of executive directors is culturally diverse: five nationalities are represented in the team of nine, namely Saudi, Yemeni, Moroccan, British and Egyptian (see Figure 6.1). The company has been hugely successful, doubling revenues from 2011–2015 and has recently been elected Employer of Choice in the Kingdom. However, because of an economic downturn, there has been a stagnation in growth. In 2014 a new CEO was appointed and more recently two new executive team members have come on board. It now seems the changing economic climate and changes in the composition of the team have caused frictions in the team. Although one of the company's main recent campaigns is called "be engaged," there are signals of individual executives being less engaged, the atmosphere in team meetings becoming less constructive, directors increasingly working in silos, and the cabinet not speaking with one voice. According to the client, interpersonal understanding and trust, interpersonal communication, collaboration and alignment are key to the effectiveness of the team. The central question with which the client approached the external consultant was: taking into consideration the team's key elements, how can we enhance the effectiveness of the leadership team?

The Research Process

Data were gathered by means of four different activities, of which the first two took place remotely (online surveys) and the last two were performed in-company:

1. Stakeholder feedback was gathered by means of a team effectiveness survey consisting of 48 Likert-scale items and eight open-ended questions.

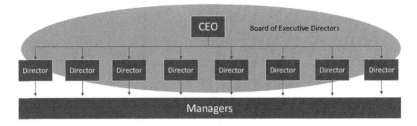

Figure 6.1 Organization Chart of the Company

The survey was completed anonymously by seven out of nine directors, and 20 managers directly reporting to the executive team. Key topics were the focus of the team (mission), efficiency in execution, internal dynamics, external relationships and the team's capacity to learn and innovate. The output was a computer-generated summary team effectiveness report.

2. A Belbin team-role assessment was conducted (Belbin, 2000) by means of a self-perception questionnaire (completed by every team member individually) and observer assessments (completed by at least four stakeholders, nominated by every director). This method focuses on the natural way a person behaves, contributes and interacts within the team, how this is perceived by the person himself or herself and by their colleagues. The output was a computer-generated individual team-role report for every director and a team report for the team as a whole.

3. Semi-structured interviews (1.5 hours each) were conducted by the consultant with all executive directors, on the key topics, including the team's performance, individual contributions of self and others, trust, collaboration and leadership. The output consisted of nine individual interview reports, written by the consultant on the basis of interview notes.

4. The consultant sat in on and observed a three-hour regular Executive Team meeting.

Timewise, this was a quite condensed project of just 16 days from start to finish (see Table 6.1).

The team effectiveness survey led to a number of insights on the team's self-image. The team saw themselves as highly results-oriented, performance-driven and focused. Top-scoring items on the survey were: "This team defines stretching goals and deliverables" (average score of all respondents 4.19 on the 5-point scale) and "This team knows the contribution it makes to corporate success" (average 4.22). The team considered themselves cohesive and well aligned around business priorities. Top-scoring items were:

Table 6.1 Timeline for Research and Intervention

Day 1	Day 2–10	Day 11	Day 12	Day 13	Day 14	Day 15–16
Participants receive online team effectiveness survey and team-role assessment	Time for participants and stakeholders to complete various questionnaires	5 interviews with Executive Team members	4 interviews with Executive Team members	Observation of Executive Team meeting Consultant's reporting time	Travel to off-site location Consultant's reporting time	Two days off-site

"This team presents a united front in public" (average 4.08) and "Team members respect and trust each other as individuals" (average 4.08). The team considered themselves less effective regarding open communication and feedback. Lowest-scoring items were: "Team members challenge each other constructively, saying what needs to be said" (average 3.15) and "Team members give each other honest, helpful feedback" (average 3.19). It should be noted that to differentiate between higher- and lower-scoring items, it was helpful not just to look at the average scores, but also consider the statistical *mode* (the answer given most frequently). For instance, on the item "Team members give each other honest, helpful feedback," the mode was 2, meaning most team members and stakeholders gave it a score of 2 on a 5-point scale.

The team perceived themselves as having some difficulty in dealing with diversity. On the open-ended questions, there were comments like: "We sometimes lack the courage to speak our minds openly when we disagree" and "The team is composed of very different, strong characters. This is what makes us a strong company, however people do not listen to each other very well, there is also blaming and not truly appreciating the differences in personality and culture."

The Belbin team-role assessment confirmed the strength of the team in results-orientation and drive. Of the nine team roles the so-called *Shaper* was strongest represented in the team; four of the nine team members had the Shaper as their primary team role. This role is defined as: "providing the necessary drive to ensure that the team keeps moving and does not lose focus or momentum" (Belbin, 2000). The Belbin team report characterized the team as follows: "This is a team that contains people high in drive and the ability to overcome obstacles. If its members can work together, it can achieve a great deal. The risk is that this energy can result in internal conflict which is not easily resolved. This team may find that members are unwilling to adjust to one another. There may be difficulty in developing a positive atmosphere. It may therefore be necessary to find someone who can strengthen morale and help the team to work harmoniously together."

Culture and cultural diversity play an important role in this company and the effectiveness of the team. The different national and organizational cultures represented in the team affect the team in a number of ways. First, diversity plays a role with regard to the leadership style of the new CEO and the way this is perceived by others. The CEO was groomed by his previous company, a large multinational FMCG company rooted in a culture of careful planning and structure and with a data-driven management setting clear objectives. His style was experienced as quite different from the existing management culture in the client company, which was more personally engaging, entrepreneurial and intuitive. This reluctance to change is in line with a recent study on personality traits of Saudi managers, who score significantly high on prudence (Bolhuis, 2016). According to the Hogan Personality Inventory, individuals with high scores on prudence tend to have difficulties in situations of management change, which may affect their overall effectiveness (Hogan & Hogan, 2007). The business language that was used turned out to be another aspect that was affected by cultural diversity. Only one team member had English as a mother tongue, yet the business discussions were supposed to be in English. This led to inequality within the team as some could express themselves with greater fluency and accuracy than others, and were also better able to understand what was being said. Similar problems surfaced in earlier research on the use of business English in an international context, with awareness raising being offered as a possible solution (Rogerson-Revell, 2007; Salario, 2012). The levels of trust and openness displayed in team discussions also testified to the team's diversity. In this particular team, the group discussions and the way in which members gave each other feedback was observed to be quite open and direct, even in the vertical relationship between director and CEO. This is not the usual pattern in Saudi Arabia, where the power distance experienced between superior and subordinate is relatively high (Hofstede, Hofstede, & Minkov, 2010). For example, it is not uncommon to find that when a superior is in the room, subordinates will be reluctant to speak. Cultural diversity further influenced the communication styles of the team members. Some individuals within the team had troublesome relationships because, from their cultural perspective, the communication style or leadership style of other members was inappropriate or even dysfunctional when the latter tried to reach consensus or solve issues together. It was remarkable that the team adopted an ethnocentric approach in this case, seeing their ethnic backgrounds as a driving force behind behaviour and thereby increasing cultural differences. For example, by his Saudi peers, the UK team member was considered to be typically results-focused, objective and phlegmatic, yet bold and even aggressive in discussions. The Saudi team members found each other more empathetic, inclusive, warm and more emotional in discussions. The communication style of the British director, which was direct and more performance-focused, was not always effective to get things done in the Saudi culture, where relationships and personal bonds are essential. The composition of the team also showed that the national culture of Saudi Arabia clearly had an impact on the executive team of this originally Saudi organization. In Saudi Arabia – although this is changing – it is still rare to see women in executive management roles. This executive team of directors, like almost all executive boards in Saudi Arabia, was composed of only men.

Consultancy and Acceptance

The research activities mentioned previously were not just diagnostics. They already were interventions that led to a more effective intercultural awareness, encouraging self-reflection and a higher level of self-awareness within the team. Following the research phase, a two-day team development programme (or so-called team retreat) was facilitated by the external consultant. The team retreat was held in a place that was literally far away from business, a conference hotel accommodation in Jordan and included the following elements. First, the results of the research were presented and the different reports were handed out. These showed how the team and the individual directors perceived themselves and how they were perceived by others. The reports also included recommendations as to how the roles in the team could best be allocated to play to the strengths of each team member. Facilitated by the consultant, conversations in pairs were organized for team members to discuss interpersonal relationships. The pairs discussed their personal styles and the team roles they brought into this setting, the way the pair work together, and in what way their styles could be complementary and create synergies between their departments. Facilitated by the consultant, team building exercises were performed based on the method of action learning. In these exercises the team had to work on a particular task together, the team's performance was observed and benchmarked against executive teams from other companies. In a debriefing discussion, areas of improvement were identified and transferred to the next exercise. In the course of the two-day programme every director had a one-hour individual feedback or coaching session with the consultant to decide on the specific strengths that director brought to the team, his potentially dysfunctional behaviour, and things he could or should do to improve and to help the team perform even better. The team retreat ended by formulating commitments and planning action. At the end of the programme a group discussion took place to formulate collective actions that the team would commit to. In addition, every team member shared his personal commitment with the rest of the team: "based on the insights from these two days, what I will do to continue to enhance the team's performance is. . . " Each team member appointed one colleague who would hold him accountable for this commitment with a check-in call or face-to-face meeting after one month.

To assess the impact of this intervention programme, the intervention was evaluated on the four different levels on which a training programme can be evaluated: the reaction level, the learning level, the behaviour level and the results level (Kirkpatrick & Kayser, 2016). These levels will be reviewed next. On the reaction level the participants themselves provided very positive verbal feedback about the diagnostic phase as well as the team retreat. The programme received an average score of 8.9 on a 10-point scale. In addition to the company-specific diagnosis and intervention, also more general aspects such as going on such a journey as a team, investing time and effort in team development, the sheer opportunity to speak confidentially about personal experiences and relationships in the team and to give and receive feedback, traveling abroad and spending time in a beautiful location in Jordan were appreciated and contributed to the positive evaluation. It is not *business as usual* for a board of directors to create such an opportunity to reflect on teamwork and internal relationships. The positive impact of creating such time and space, in itself, should not be underestimated. On the learning level, the team survey and team role assessment, supported by the experiential learning exercises, ensured that participants received extremely rich feedback on their contribution and behaviour in the team, as well as constructive ideas about what they could improve individually and collectively. They gained insight about themselves and about their colleagues, and learned how their team benchmarked against other executive teams in similar circumstances. On the behaviour level, a verbal follow-up evaluation with the HR Director three months after the team retreat suggested that the internal dynamics and cooperation within the team had improved significantly. Without any cracks in their reputation, they had achieved a major business acquisition, which is usually a process that puts strain on a team and can lead to conflict and misalignment. According to the HR Director: "Since the team retreat, we have not had a single dysfunctional discussion or conflict. People speak out much more openly in team meetings than before. And whenever there are new responsibilities or tasks to assign, we take a look at our team role analysis and allocate roles so that everyone can 'play to strength'." The fourth and final level, that of results, is the most difficult to evaluate because there are many other aspects that influence the company's business performance. Although the team members were positive about the results in the previously mentioned acquisition process, it cannot be concluded that this is due to the intervention described here.

Final Reflection

Several factors contributed to the success of this intervention. The consultant occupied the position of a neutral outsider and was therefore seen as objective and fair, eliciting a high degree of mutual trust. The CEO stressed that intercultural differences should not hinder effective collaboration, and set an example by being open to feedback and taking opportunities to improve himself. The CEO furthermore created a safe learning environment, by reassuring the directors that their individual roles were highly valued and that this executive team would stay in place for some time to come. Another aspect is the co-authorship of the programme of client and consultant together, which prevented participants from feeling they were acted upon, rather than acting. Without this co-authorship, participants might not have been committed to the outcomes. Lastly, intercultural stereotypes were not used and intercultural differences were not named as such. The focus was just on differences between people instead of ethnicity and on how to make best use of these differences by a positive framing of differences and by using the positive and reinforcing language of team roles, applying the principle of playing to strength (Maznevski, 1994). Rather than the ethnocentric attitude which the team previously adopted, they now displayed a more ethnorelative perspective, which is an important condition of intercultural effectiveness (Bennett, 2004). Religious values and governmental regulations are sensitive issues which are as difficult to address in the context of a team development programme as in this case study. For example, due to the Saudi Arabian labour system, Saudi nationals have a stronger position in terms of job security than their non-Saudi colleagues. It is much more difficult for an employer to fire a Saudi national than to fire an expatriate. The inequality between Saudi and non-Saudi board members and the fact that the position of non-Saudis is less secure is not openly discussed in the workplace, and has a negative impact on trust and cohesion within a culturally diverse team.

References

Belbin, R. M. (2000). *Beyond the team* (1st ed.). Oxford: Butterworth-Heinemann.

Bennett, M. J. (2004). Becoming interculturally competent. In J. S. Wurzel (Ed.), *Toward multiculturalism: A reader in multicultural education* (pp. 62–77). Newton, MA: Intercultural Resource Corporation. Retrieved from www.idrinstitute.org/wp-content/uploads/2018/02/becoming_ic_competent.pdf

Bolhuis, J. C. (2016). *Interculturele competenties onder Saoedische managers* (Unpublished master's thesis). Utrecht University, Utrecht, The Netherlands. Retrieved from http://dspace.library.uu.nl/handle/1874/338990

Hofstede, G., Hofstede, G. J., & Minkov, M. (2010). *Cultures and organizations: Software of the mind* (3rd rev. ed.). New York, NY: McGraw-Hill.

Hogan, R., & Hogan, J. (2007). *Hogan personality inventory manual*. Hogan Assessment Systems. Retrieved from www.mentis.international/assets/04019_hpi_tm_secure.pdf

Kirkpatrick, J., & Kayser, W. (2016). *Kirkpatrick's four levels of training evaluation*. Alexandria, VA: ATD Press.

Maznevski, M. L. (1994). Understanding our differences: Performance in decision-making groups with diverse members. *Human Relations, 47*(5), 531–552.

Rogerson-Revell, P. (2007). Using English for international business: A European case study. *English for Specific Purposes, 26,* 103–120.

Salario, T. (2012). *Adjusting to non-native speaker levels of English: Attitudes of native speakers of English* (Unpublished master's thesis). Utrecht University, Utrecht, The Netherlands. Retrieved from http://dspace.library.uu.nl/handle/1874/241034

Part III
Education

Case Study 7

Advising Parents on Bilingual Education of Their Children

Manuela Pinto

Introduction

Experts in intercultural communication may be asked to give advice about raising children bilingually. Everyday life provides massive evidence that children can easily cope with two or more languages. Yet, when the decision has to be taken about their own offspring, parents are in doubt: "Will two languages confuse my child?", "Will my child have a language delay?". Research in the last two decades has shown that learning two languages does not jeopardize children's cognitive and linguistic development (Serratrice, 2013). However, parental concern about this issue is multi-layered. It is the intercultural communication expert's task to address these concerns one by one, offering research-based information, providing parents with the knowledge they need to take their own decisions. This chapter presents a consultancy case study that specifically addresses the linguistic aspects of intercultural society: it concerns children growing up with two languages. This case clearly shows the relevant competencies of an intercultural expert and the way in which these can be employed to improve intercultural communication.

The Case

It is natural, and for some people it is the only option, to use their mother tongue when communicating with their children. The first language is the language learnt in childhood, the language of affections, of emotions. How could parents possibly use a different language to address their children? Yet other people may show some irritation when hearing parents address their children in a language they do not understand. Although research has shown that raising children bilingually has no negative effects, still not only laypeople but also professionals fear that using a minority language will damage the development of the community language, in this specific case Dutch. This explains parents' reluctance to raise their children with two languages.

Working in second language acquisition research brings us researchers in contact with bilingual families (mixed marriages, expatriates, migrants).[1] They all use some form of bilingual policy in raising their children. As long as the children are young and spend a great deal of time in the family, this is not a problem. However, as soon as the children start going to school, social pressure increases and parents start feeling insecure about their bilingual educational choices. After discussing these issues with many parents, it became clear to us that sceptical voices about bilingualism often originate in a lack of information about this phenomenon. We then decided to instigate knowledge dissemination initiatives to enable bilingual families to make informed choices among alternatives. The present chapter describes the steps that were taken in the context of BIMU (Bi/Multilingualism at Utrecht) to develop consultancy for parents wanting to raise their children with two languages.

Parents had two main questions:

a. Will two languages confuse my child?
b. Will two languages provide a language delay?

Before addressing these questions, we thought it was important to determine our clients' profile (cultural background and socio-economic status) and their motivation for raising their children bilingually. Our clients were mostly young mixed families, migrants and expats that had recently moved to the Netherlands. It is important to note that their socio-economic status (SES) ranged from middle to high. Most of these people had an academic degree and spoke English. Therefore, communication outside the home was never problematic. These people were knowledgeable about bilingualism and were conscious of their right to keep alive their mother tongue. However, they felt insecure about possible negative consequences for their children at a cognitive level. Although raising a child bilingually is becoming more common in the Netherlands, parents are aware that this is not the norm and feel that they have to justify their choice. What our clients requested was recent, research-based information in order to have sound arguments to justify their bilingual choice. However, we thought it was also important to know the reasons for these parents for wanting to pass their minority language on to their children. In our view the motivational aspect of bilingual education is often neglected, which interferes with a mutual understanding between its advocates and its opponents. An intercultural communication expert, particularly in his or her role as mediator, should be aware of the reasons parents have for wanting to teach their own language to their children. As Blom (2015) shows in a survey he conducted with participants in the Growing Up Bilingual workshops at Utrecht University, parents want their children to be able to communicate with family members that only speak the minority language. They also want their children to get access to the minority culture, as part of their mixed identity. Competence in the minority language may help them to achieve these goals. On the other hand, professionals, policymakers and members of the dominant language community are prone to focus on practical issues like mutual intelligibility, academic success and smooth integration in the host country. We believe it is the task of an ICC expert to take into account the concerns and the wishes of both parties and, most important, to make them explicit in order to reach understanding and collaboration.

The second stage of our study consisted in re-phrasing our clients' questions into clear research questions. In this specific case we followed the steps reported here:

a. Identification of the problem:
    Clients worry about their children's language development, more specifically, about confusion in production of speech and delay in the acquisition process.
b. Identification of the symptoms:
    Code switching, which may indicate confusion and an inability to learn two languages properly (hence, delay compared to monolingual peers).
c. (More precise) question: is code switching a symptom of erroneous use of the languages and/or of lack of competence?

This stage was a crucial part of the consultancy. The consultant needs academic skills to pin down the clients' questions, since this topic concerns children's welfare and it may be quite emotional for parents to deal with it. The consultant needs a sound background in language development and language use, as it will be his or her unique task to integrate information from different relevant areas of bilingual acquisition research and provide the clients with a complete picture of the situation. We examined parents' reports and made an inventory of their concerns, such as "*My child mixes up the two languages, makes up words using the grammar of both languages*". We first tried to determine the common denominator of these complaints and we identified code switching as the clearest symptom. Code switching is normally considered an indicator of poor language proficiency, despite the fact that more than four decades of linguistic research has shown that switching has a functional role and requires instead a high level of linguistic competence (Appel & Muysken, 2006). The distinction between language competence and language use brought us to the formulation of a specific research question:

Is code switching a symptom of erroneous use of the languages and/or of lack of competence?

The Research Process

The research question makes explicit the goals of this case: informing our clients about the implications of code switching for language competence and language use in young bilinguals. The information we wanted to provide is based on research and corroborated by empirical evidence. To this purpose, we conducted a literature review about code switching, specifically focusing on studies examining the use of languages (the functional aspect) and studies examining the development of two distinct grammars (the competence aspect) in young children.

First of all, we tried to determine the type of information we needed to provide a convincing answer to the research question. If code switching were the result of an erroneous use of the two languages, utterances containing code switching might be unintelligible. This does not seem to be the case. Lanza's (1997, 2001) studies on code switching in early bilinguals provide evidence for a functional use of mixing in the production of young bilingual children from the age of two. Lanza shows that children identify specific cues in the parental input that provide them with information about the linguistic preferences of their interlocutor. Thus, scientific research provides evidence for the claim that not only do young bilinguals use code switching in a functional way, they also appear to be sensitive to the properties of the input they receive and they are able to adapt their own speech to those properties.

We turned then to examining grammar development in young bilinguals. If code switching were an indicator of poor linguistic competence, bilingual speech would show violations of sentence grammar and grammar development would be seriously delayed in these children. However, as argued by Werker and Byers-Heinlein (2008), bilingual language development is typically within the monolingual range for most aspects. Meisel (2001), among others, shows that by the time they acquire syntactic structure (around the age of two), bilinguals know the word order patterns available in the languages they speak and do not mix them up. Particularly revealing in this respect are MacSwan's (2000) and Cantone's (2007) studies which systematically analyse the structure of young bilinguals' mixed utterances and show that they all obey sentence structure rules.

This brief literature review supports the claim that code switching in young bilinguals is not to be seen as symptomatic of a lack of language competence or of poor understanding of language use. In other words, code switching is a familiar feature in bilingual speech and it reveals good language competence and high sensitivity for language variation and language use.

Consultancy and Acceptance

The advice of an intercultural communication expert does a number of things:

- It fits the profile of the audience (in terms of level of education and in terms of socio-economic status)
- It gives a clear analysis of the problem, identifying a number of issues and their relevance to the situation as a whole
- It provides an answer based on research
- It makes explicit different parties' expectations
- It informs, but it does not prescribe
- It attempts to combine insights from different research areas

Questions of the kind discussed earlier are very common among bilinguals and people are eager to share their (positive or negative) experiences on raising children bilingually. We decided that our advice could be best given in the form of a workshop consisting of three parts: a general part in which we discuss parents' questions on a specific topic and for which we provide evidence-based research; a discussion session during which the audience is divided into subgroups and discusses specific themes; and finally a short plenary session in which we report the main findings and are available for questions. At all stages, the advisory role of the intercultural expert requires integration of research-based information on language acquisition with knowledge of cultural diversity. We started providing workshops in 2010 and since then the many participants have appreciated the information we provide. Every year newcomers join our mailing list and register for activities. A survey we have recently run among the participants of one of our workshops resulted in a positive evaluation of the programme (Blom, 2015). However, Blom also made a few recommendations. The one that struck us most was the request for more depth and details in the linguistic issues we present.

Final Reflection

We believe it is the prerogative of an intercultural communication expert to provide advice on intercultural matters combining linguistic expertise with social and culture-specific aspects like background, norms and values and linguistic and cultural identity of the people involved. In the above case linguistic competence occupies a central position. However, it would be short-sighted not to consider other aspects of the problem, like the clients' profile or their motivation for maintaining their mother tongue. The unique task of an intercultural communication expert is to use insights from research to tackle real-life issues in intercultural communication.

Note

1 In 2010 Ivana Brasileiro, Manuela Pinto, and Sharon Unsworth initiated a number of activities aimed to raise awareness and understanding about bilingual education. Since then, they have provided a number of workshops on growing up with two or more languages and created a digital platform offering research based information on many topics involving bilingualism.

References

Appel, R., & Muysken, P. (2006). *Language contact and bilingualism*. Amsterdam: Amsterdam University Press.

Blom, L. (2015). *Twee talen, één gedachte? Een kwalitatief onderzoek naar de beoordeling en efficiëntie van de workshop 'growing up bilingual' en de samenstelling en beweegredenen van haar deelnemers* (Unpublished master's thesis). Utrecht University, Utrecht, The Netherlands.

Cantone, K. F. (2007). *Code switching in bilingual children* (Vol. 2). Dordrecht: Springer.

Lanza, E. (1997). Language contact in bilingual two-year-olds and code-switching: Language encounters of a different kind? *International Journal of Bilingualism, 1*(2), 135–162.

Lanza, E. (2001). Bilingual first language acquisition: A discourse perspective on language contact in parent-child interaction. In J. Cenoz & F. Genesee (Eds.), *Trends in bilingual acquisition* (pp. 201–230). Amsterdam: John Benjamins Publishing Company.

MacSwan, J. (2000). The architecture of the bilingual language faculty: Evidence from intrasentential code switching. *Bilingualism: Language and Cognition, 3*(1), 37–54.

Meisel, I. M. (2001). The simultaneous acquisition of two first languages. In J. Cenoz & F. Genesee (Eds.), *Trends in bilingual acquisition* (pp. 11–43). Amsterdam: John Benjamins Publishing Company.

Serratrice, L. (2013). The bilingual child. In T. K. Bhatia & W. C. Ritchie (Eds.), *The handbook of bilingualism and multilingualism* (2nd ed., pp. 85–108). Chichester: John Wiley & Sons, Ltd.

Werker, J. F., & Byers-Heinlein, K. (2008). Bilingualism in infancy: First steps in perception and comprehension. *Trends in Cognitive Sciences, 12*(4), 144–151.

Case Study 8

Advising Linguistically Diverse Schools on Developing a School-wide Language Policy

Koen Van Gorp and Pandora Versteden

The Case

In response to a growing linguistically diverse student population, schools in Flanders (Belgium) are looking for research-based answers to questions they have about language acquisition, developing the language of schooling and multilingualism. In 2008, all primary schools that are part of the educational network of Catholic schools in the city of Genk (i.e., the school district *De Speling*) approached the Centre for Language and Education (CLE) of the University of Leuven (KU Leuven) to enquire about consultancy and support precisely about these topics.

In Flemish primary education, L1 Dutch speakers and L2 Dutch learners (i.e., students who mainly speak a language other than the language of instruction at home) share a classroom and are taught the same curriculum. In the Flemish Region, on average one out of five students in primary education are L2 learners; in Genk the average is 28.4% (Lokale Inburgerings- en Integratiemonitor, 2016). In the schools of *De Speling*, the average is 25.7%. A large group of L1 and L2 Dutch speakers, especially those from parents with a lower socioeconomic background, still underachieves in the Flemish educational system. National and international studies indicate that these groups of learners are particularly vulnerable (Organization for Economic Cooperation and Development, 2006). Attaining the Flemish education standards for these groups of learners proves to be difficult (Steunpunt toetsontwikkeling en peilingen, 2014). This vulnerability is attributed at least in part to their lack of opportunities to acquire the language of schooling (Belfi et al., 2011). To encourage the use of Dutch, most Flemish primary schools adhere to a restrictive language policy on the use of the students' home languages at school, often both in the classroom and at the playground. School teams are open to changing their restrictive language policy but have questions about how to do so and are anxious about some of the consequences of allowing or even creating space for the students' home languages (Strobbe et al., 2017).

From 1991 to 2000, the school district that consulted the CLE received support from a specialized educational network (OVGB – Onderwijsvoor-rangsgebiedenbeleid Limburg). OVGB helped the schools in the province of Limburg to organize proficiency-based language teaching in order to support the development of the language of schooling. After 2000, the schools had to fall back on the pedagogical support provided by their regular educational network within the Flemish educational system. However, the school district felt that this (free of cost) pedagogical support system could not support school teams in enough depth and breadth to implement pedagogical change addressing these language-in-education issues throughout the school team. They were looking for extra support from a specialized organization like the CLE.

The CLE was established in 1990 precisely to support schools in developing the language of schooling (i.e., Dutch as an academic register) and has been working with schools and teachers ever since on topics like task-based language teaching, powerful learning environments, content-based language teaching, language-in-education policies and multilingualism (e.g., Van den Branden, 2006; Van Gorp, 2018). The CLE responded positively and started an in-depth conversation with the president of the school board, and the superintendent and pedagogical director of the school district. These initial conversations led to a long-term plan unique in the Flemish educational context. The idea was to start a three-year trajectory to develop a school language or language-in-education policy that focuses on creating powerful (language) learning environments across the schools, classes and subjects. The aim of the language policy was to advance students' proficiency in the academic register and create a space where speakers with different home languages feel welcome and respected. The president and superintendent did not only want to start a pedagogical project focused on creating powerful language learning environments, but they also wanted to evaluate the effects of implementing such a change in their school district. In consultation with the school board and all principals of *De Speling*, all stakeholders decided to roll out this comprehensive language policy stepwise starting with the teachers of Kindergarten (K1–K3) and then, from 2012 onward, systematically expanding the project to Grade 1–6: introducing the project to Grade 1 in 2012, adding Grade 2 in 2013, etc. The potential disadvantages of implementing this language policy incrementally were that it would engage the schools in a long-term innovation and could create an innovation fatigue along the way. In addition, it would take time to see improvement in students' school success throughout their primary school trajectory. The advantages were setting up an in-depth process with a smaller group of teachers (i.e., a group of school-internal coaches (see later on in the chapter) and a group of teachers teaching the same grades across the school district) so that all teachers' voices could be heard, and allowing for continuous feedback and adjustments further down the line. Such a long-term project was of particular interest to the CLE. It allowed the CLE to implement its ideas about pedagogical innovations in a large school district, build relationships with different stakeholders, involve the voice of all stakeholders in shaping the ongoing project, and by doing so, it was hoped, overcome resistance to pedagogical change observed in other similar but more short-term projects across Flanders. Furthermore, the research project provided an opportunity to collect longitudinal data on teachers' beliefs and practices, and on students' learning outcomes. Giving shape to such a profound pedagogical and research project in partnership with a school board, principals and teachers was a first for the CLE. The CLE assigned this task to one of her most experienced consultants. She acted as the main consultant. Two other CLE consultants supported the main consultant part-time. The main CLE consultant guiding this process could build on her expertise in shaping this project but also had to figure out how to apply the CLE's language policy and implementation framework in this new, complex context.

The Research Process

In a first phase of the project, the CLE and the school board and principals discussed how a shared sense of urgency and vision could be established in order to get all Kindergarten teachers involved and realize lasting effects. Data on language proficiency tests were gathered and analysed, CLE consultants observed classroom practices, and a questionnaire was administered to the school team to identify what the Kindergarten teachers perceived as the most important problems their students face learning the language of schooling. Based on this information (i.e., baseline data), the CLE, the president, superintendent and pedagogical director decided to focus on oral language skills and on creating a powerful language environment in each classroom that would allow children to develop their Dutch language skills during every moment of the day ("all day long"). The idea of a powerful (language) learning environment was represented in the figure of three circles (Verhelst, 2006): creating a positive and safe climate (outer circle) in which children perform meaningful tasks (middle circle) and are provided with interactional support to accomplish these tasks (inner circle) (see Figure 8.1).

The school board hired school-internal coaches to support the implementation of the powerful learning environment in Kindergarten. The coaches' task was not to support the students, but to support the teachers in creating powerful learning environments in their classrooms. These school-internal coaches were themselves coached by the main CLE consultant. The CLE consultant introduced them to the concepts of task-based language education

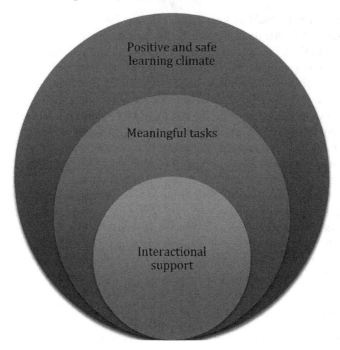

Figure 8.1 Three Circles of a Powerful Learning Environment

(e.g., the three circles) and trained their coaching skills. The CLE consultant also reached out to all the Kindergarten teachers in the school district by organizing professional development opportunities focusing on task-based education and on their teaching skills to support the language of schooling, and to the school principals by focusing on the development and implementation of a language-in-education policy.

During the first year, and all consecutive years, data were gathered to address the following questions:

1. What are the effects of the intervention on the students' language development as evidenced in oral language proficiency tests?
2. How do the teachers' perceptions with respect to the project evolve? Do teachers develop a deeper understanding of the project's key concepts (i.e., school language policy, task-based education, powerful learning environment)? Do teaching practices become more powerful as evidenced by behaviour linked to the three circles?
3. How do the school-internal coaches' perceptions with respect to the project evolve? Do coaches develop a deeper understanding of the project's

key concepts (i.e., school language policy, task-based education, powerful learning environment)? Do coaching practices become more powerful and efficient?

In consultation, a fourth research question was added in the second phase of the project (i.e., moving into Grade 1 of primary school):

4. Do the schools develop and implement a school-wide language-in-education policy? Do schools pursue a policy that supports the school-internal coaches (and therefore also teachers) to target the objectives of the project?

The idea was that all three/four legs of the research study were interconnected. To realize real change, findings in all four domains had to move in the anticipated direction.

This study required a vast amount of data collection and analysis. Data collection consisted of language tests, classroom observations, interviews and surveys. Data analyses were quantitative and qualitative looking for meaningful connections between all data findings and interpreting the data in function of the interventions by the ELC consultants, the school-internal coaches and the teachers.

A recurrent concern in the conversations between the school district's stakeholders and the CLE was the budget to finance both the pedagogical and research part of this project. As the main CLE consultant was a primary school teacher herself, the school board decided to hire her part-time. For her other part-time, the CLE consultant was on the payroll of the university. Hiring the consultant as a teacher saved the school board money, and allowed both partners to keep collaborating and executing this ambitious project. This meant that the interactions with the coaches and the professional development opportunities with other teachers were provided by the CLE consultant in her capacity as a colleague, whereas the CLE consultant conducted the research study as a university employee. To downsize the costs of the research further, the pedagogical director gathered all test data from the teachers. These data were inputted in a spreadsheet by student teachers working for the school district. Involving school district employees in the research was an interesting turn of events. It necessitated detailed conversations with all participants on data collection and a careful follow-up of all the steps involved in the data collection by the CLE consultant. The result was that the pedagogical director and the superintendent became quite knowledgeable in organizing a research study, something that proved very valuable in the course of this long-term partnership. Whereas the data collection and analyses continued from 2012 to 2014 (adding Grade 1–3), the school board questioned the value of the research project for the following school years (from 2015 onward; adding Grade 4–6). Actually, the school board wanted to downsize the cost of the project. Acknowledging the value of the pedagogical part of the project, they were less convinced to continue the research part. They believed the study would not necessarily provide future relevant insights into the language development of the students, or into teachers and coaches' perceptions and practices. In those discussions, the superintendent and pedagogical director turned out to be the most fervent defenders of the empirical study.

Consultancy and Acceptance

The consultancy and implementation process were informed by the following guiding principles (see Berben, 2012; Kotter, 2007; Van den Branden, 2009):

• Create a sense of urgency and a shared vision and ambition based on recognition of teachers' concerns and addressing teachers' perceived problems;
• Create a "powerful guiding coalition" that supports and articulates this vision and ambition across the school team (i.e., the superintendent, pedagogical director and the school-internal coaches);
• Define concrete, feasible and thus easy-to-implement goals and actions that meet the ambition and vision of the school and by doing so creating a shared language to talk about the innovation (e.g., the three circles) and creating short-term wins for the teachers;
• Provide support throughout the implementation process, e.g., by providing hands-on workshops in which teachers are presented with and develop themselves activities and tools that help them to implement the innovative actions in their classrooms, and by coaching the teachers. By involving the teachers a sense of ownership is created;
• Evaluate the effects of the actions using standardized tests to inform the school team about the students' progress in acquiring the language of schooling. Use these findings to assess the success of the shared ambition and vision, and actions;
• Create opportunities for coaches, teachers and principals to interact and continue the conversation about the innovation.

Putting these principles in practice required intensive communication between all major stakeholders, especially because we were implementing these principles on a larger scale, not just within one school team, but across the school teams of a large school district. The CLE consultants spent much time consulting with the superintendent and pedagogical director, and interacting with and training the school-internal coaches on a monthly basis. The CLE consultants also organized, together with the school-internal coaches, workshops (2–3 per school year), called *How?So!days*, for teachers teaching a particular grade. The advantage of having workshops across the school district was that teachers from the different schools could exchange experiences, tips and tricks. The fact that colleagues teaching the same age groups wrestled with the same issues and that they were looking for answers to similar questions had a positive effect on the interest for and backing of the project among teachers. The fact that schools across the school district shared a vision and ambition created a sense of unity. However, it also allowed schools to translate this vision and ambition to their own context, allowing for a school-specific narrative as well. This process was supported by the fact that the main CLE consultant was available and accessible to all stakeholders. This created the feeling in all actors that she was not just an expert brought in from the outside to tell them how to teach and organize their classrooms and schools. On the contrary, the CLE consultant was becoming very quickly an insider; an insider who all actors trusted and who they could rely on for their professional development and for guiding the innovation to the classroom floor. Evaluations of the *How?So!days* revealed that throughout the multi-year project the teachers really appreciated the fact that the workshops allowed them to share success experiences, that they received many practical teaching ideas and tips, and that the workshops engaged the teachers in a very positive way, creating positive pressure to take risks and try innovative actions (like co-teaching, content-based language teaching, project work across subjects) in their classroom (Loman, Versteden, Moons, & Van Gorp, 2015). Still, the whole process met with the resistance that is well documented in the implementation of innovation. In the 2011 and 2015 evaluation, some of the coaches indicated that they felt insecure, not yet ready to coach their teacher colleagues and did not always know how to reach out to especially older colleagues who were sceptical of the innovation and showed resistance to the project (Loman, De Roo, Wijckmans, Schuytn, & Verhelst, 2011; Loman et al., 2015).

This relationship of trust helped the CLE consultant considerably in discussing the research results with all stakeholders in 2011 (Kindergarten) and 2015 (K-3). Before officially communicating the results to all stakeholders, the findings were discussed with the superintendent and pedagogical director. These discussions helped to determine the focus of the wider communication and to contextualize certain results. These preparatory discussions and the actual discussions during the presentations of the research findings to all teachers in the school district helped shape the recommendations for action during the next school year(s).

Some of the recommendations of the 2011 evaluation aimed at keeping the project going and keeping all teachers and coaches involved. The study confirmed that transforming teachers' beliefs and practices was a long-term endeavour and that the coaching skills of the school-internal coaches required more training. Although progress had been made with respect to teachers' beliefs and practices, especially with respect to creating a positive and safe climate (i.e., the outer circle), more sustained support and innovative experiences were needed with respect to the implementation of meaningful tasks and interactional support (the other two circles). The study also revealed that teachers felt uncomfortable with allowing the home languages of the students at school. The topics *home languages* together with *meaningful tasks* and *interactional support* became the focus of the project's next phase for Kindergarten teachers (2012–2015). Interestingly, the findings of the 2011 evaluation report were largely confirmed in the 2015 report. Having teachers use meaningful language learning tasks in their classroom and scaffold students' learning through interaction remained a challenge. Not only did the primary school teachers go through the same struggle as the Kindergarten teachers implementing both, but also Kindergarten teachers' practices still showed room for improvement, especially designing meaningful tasks. The 2015 report indicated overall progress with respect to the position of the student's home languages at school. Teachers showed more tolerance toward the use of the students' home languages. However, the survey and interviews revealed that there was still no shared vision across the school teams, especially in Grades 1–3, in the different schools with respect to this topic. Finally, the 2015 study confirmed that the role of the school-internal coaches was key in bringing about change in teachers' beliefs and practices. However, from the start, these coaches were not professional coaches, but teachers that responded to an internal call for coaches by the school principals. The transformation from teacher to coach took time and training, and depended on the one hand on the personality of the coach, on the other hand on the practice opportunities the coaches had in their school. Having an external partner, the CLE consultant, who had a great deal of coaching experience, turned out to be crucial in helping teachers transition into the role of school-internal coaches. Additionally, in the course of the project's second phase, the pedagogical director started to take up a bigger role in coaching the coaches allowing for a gradual phasing out of the CLE support.

Final Reflection

Collaborating with a school district for a long-term project proved to be an interesting and fruitful experience for the CLE and its consultants. Unique was the combination of a pedagogical and research project that allowed the main CLE consultant not only to work in a very close relationship with many different actors but also to monitor and adjust her actions based on actual data. The CLE consultant was both insider (a colleague of the teachers and school-internal coaches) and outsider (a researcher from the university). Being able to navigate that position and use it accordingly turned out to be valuable in moving the project along. Including actors, like the superintendent and the pedagogical director, in the organization of all parts of the project proved to be an asset as well. Creating a shared ambition and vision for the schools benefited from the trust relationships that were established over time. Notwithstanding the fact that these relationships were based on loyalty and trust, they remained professional all the time. This professional relationship and, in the end, as an outsider being able to act as a sounding board providing clear advice based on data linked with personal experiences, proved to be a very important impetus to keep the project and the innovation going.

References

Belfi, B., Cortois, L., Moons, C., Van Damme, J., Van den Branden, K., Van Gorp, K., . . . Verhelst, M. (2011). *Eindrapport OBPWO 09.04. Vorderingen van leerlingen in het leren van het Nederlands*. Leuven: KU Leuven.

Berben, M. (2012). Hoe een taalbeleid het beleidsvoerend vermogen van je school kan verhogen. *Impuls*, *43*, 2, 88–98.

Kotter, J. P. (2007). *Leading change. Why transformation efforts fail*. Cambridge, MA: Harvard Business School Press.

Lokale inburgerings- en integratiemonitor. (2016). Retrieved November 30, 2017, from http://aps.vlaanderen.be/lokaal/integratiemonitor.html

Loman, F., De Roo, B., Wijckmans, B., Schuytn, V., & Verhelst, M. (2011). *Evaluatieonderzoek Kleutertaal in scholengemeenschap De Speling – Genk. Intern rapport*. Leuven: Centrum voor Taal en Onderwijs, KU Leuven.

Loman, F., Versteden, P., Moons, C., & Van Gorp, K. (2015). *Iedereen Taalt. Effectonderzoek naar implementatie van principes van krachtige taalleeromgevingen door schoolinterne coaches in de scholengemeenschap De Speling – Genk. Intern rapport*. Leuven: Centrum voor Taal en Onderwijs, KU Leuven.

Organization for Economic Cooperation and Development (OECD). (2006). *Where immigrant students succeed: A comparative review of performance and engagement in PISA 2003*. Paris: OECD.

Steunpunt toetsontwikkeling en peilingen. (2014). *Peiling Nederlands. Lezen en luisteren in het basisonderwijs*. Brussel: Ministerie van Onderwijs en Vorming.

Strobbe, L., Van Der Wildt, A., Van Avermaet, P., Van Gorp, K., Van den Branden, K., & Van Houtte, M. (2017). How school teams perceive and handle multilingualism: The impact of a school's pupil composition. *Teaching and Teacher Education*, *64*, 93–104. doi:10.1016/j.tate.2017.01.023

Van den Branden, K. (2006). *Task-based language education: From theory to practice*. Cambridge: Cambridge University Press.

Van den Branden, K. (2009). Diffusion and implementation of innovations. In M. H. Long & C. J. Doughty (Eds.), *The handbook of language teaching* (pp. 659–672). Malden, MA: Wiley-Blackwell.

Van Gorp, K. (2018). Task-based language assessment for L1 and L2 learners in primary education: Designing a useful task-specification framework. In J. M. Davis, J. Norris, M. Malone, T. McKay, & Y. A. Son (Eds.), *Useful assessment and evaluation in language education* (pp. 131–148). Washington, DC: Georgetown University.

Verhelst, M. (2006). A box full of feelings: Promoting infants' second language acquisition all day long. In K. Van den Branden (Ed.), *Task-based language education: From theory to practice* (pp. 197–216). Cambridge: Cambridge University Press.

Case Study 9

Shifting From a Monolingual to a Plurilingual Pedagogical Practice

Marie-Paule Lory

The Case

In an age of transnational mobility, schools all over the world see an increasing number of pupils speaking different languages at home, in their communities and at school. As a result, some teachers express concerns about having to navigate through a plurilingual and a multicultural environment while supporting the development of their pupils' academic skills. The Ministry of Education (MOE) of the province of Ontario (Canada) and the East of Ottawa School Board (CEPEO) mandated me to offer for teachers in French schools a series of workshops on teaching strategies with a focus on developing oral competences among learners. The present case study describes how the workshops were structured and how they enabled participating teachers to shift their practice from a monolingual paradigm to a plurilingual one.

According to the 2016 census, two in five Canadian children have an immigrant background (Statistique Canada, 2017). Statistics Canada also predicts that children with an immigrant background could grow to represent between 39% and 49% of Canada's total child population by 2036. Thus, linguistic and cultural diversity has become a defining feature of today and tomorrow's Canadian school system. Pedagogical approaches that leverage this linguistic and cultural diversity have been shown to have a positive impact on pupils, not only at a cognitive level but also at a social and an emotional level (Armand, Dagenais, & Nicollin, 2008; Candelier, 2003; Cummins, 2007; Svalberg, 2009). Yet, the school system is still rooted in a monolingual paradigm (Cummins, 2001; Flores & Rosa, 2015; Gogolin, 1994). Among the pedagogical approaches that have been successfully implemented in school systems, "l'éveil aux langues" (Awakening to languages, CARAP, 2012) is an innovative pedagogical programme anchored in the Language Awareness movement introduced in England by Hawkins in the 1980s. Widely implemented in Europe, a "l'éveil aux langues" project was developed in 2002 in two Canadian provinces: British Columbia and Quebec (www.

elodil.umontreal.ca) and is currently adapted in two major cities (Toronto and Ottawa) in Canada's largest province, Ontario. This programme aims to empower pupils by leveraging cultural and linguistic diversity in classrooms and promotes inclusive pedagogical practices to engage pupils in reflection about cultures and languages: the language(s) of instruction, languages that pupils may speak or hear at home or in their communities and more widely, languages around the world (Lory & Armand, 2016).

It is worth noticing that although Canada has two official languages, among the 10 provinces of the country only New Brunswick is a bilingual province. Quebec's official language has been French (only) since 1969, and English is, for most of the provinces, the dominant language. In the case of Ontario, English is spoken by a large majority while French is spoken by a minority. As Canada has two official languages, the Canadian Charter of Rights and Freedoms (1982, s. 23[1]) allows for pupils with a parent who had studied in a francophone institution in Canada to enroll in French-language public or Catholic schools. More recently, policies in the admission of pupils in French-language schools in Ontario[2] changed to accept more pupils from diverse ethnic backgrounds (Cavanagh, Cammarata, & Blain, 2016). In the province of Ontario with 82 public school boards, 70 are anglophone and 12 are francophone. For French-language school boards that promote an official minority language in a context of linguistic and cultural diversity, such diversity may appear as a threat to the sustainability of the French culture and language (Gérin-Lajoie, 2008; Leurebourg, 2013). Ontario school policies are likely to maintain a monoglossic paradigm that often insists on the exclusion of languages other than French, the language of instruction (Fleuret, Bangou, & Ibrahim, 2013). Therefore, pupils may be torn between the different languages they speak or are in contact with and cannot easily embrace their plurilingualism and pluri-identities. At the end of 2016, I (the author) was asked by an agent from the Ministry of Education for the French-language schools in Ontario to offer workshops in three different parts of the province to teachers, school boards' pedagogical consultants and school directors on ways to support their pupils in developing French oral skills. Although I was new in Ontario, I was approached by the Ministry of Education based on my various experiences in training teachers in Quebec to develop pupils' oral skills and based on my new position as a University of Toronto professor. At this stage, the Ministry of Education was not considering to incorporate in our reflexions my main domain of research: Awareness of Language and more widely, the plurilingual paradigm in Education. Keeping in mind the specific context of French-language schools in Ontario, I offered these three full-day workshops on the development of French oral skills from a plurilingual and pluricultural point of view. Further, with the help of different experts from the Ministry of Education, we created four learning clips that were made available on one of the Ministry of Education websites (http://apprendreenseignerinnover.ca). We are currently working on a French oral assessment grid that will include plurilingual competences. After these first workshops, a growing interest from the participants allowed me to train more and more educators on plurilingual approaches in different conferences held by the Ministry of Education. In fact, between 2016 and 2018, I trained over 300 educators on how to adopt a plurilingual paradigm in their practices, implementing projects like "l'éveil aux langues". This specific case will be discussed in the following sections.

The Research Process

As stated earlier, even though the majority of the researchers agree on the benefits of implementing plurilingual and pluricultural pedagogical approaches in the classroom, the French school system in Ontario is still very protective of the culture and language of instruction at the exclusion of linguistic and cultural diversity (Fleuret et al., 2013; Prasad, 2012). In fact, the diversity of languages and cultures, and particularly the presence of the English language, is often seen as dangerous to the sustainability of French language and culture (Gérin-Lajoie, 2008).

Keeping in mind this particular context and the fact that, as Blommaert, Collins, and Slembrouck (2005) have argued, communicative competence is not a problem of the speaker per se, but rather refers to the (in)ability to draw on expertise within a specific context, I refined my mandate from the Ministry of Education of Ontario by examining two main questions:

1. How can teachers, pedagogical counselors and school directors be convinced of the benefits of a plurilingual and pluricultural pedagogical approach?
2. How can teachers, pedagogical counselors and school directors be supported in implementing plurilingual and pluricultural pedagogical approaches in their classrooms?

I adopted an ethnographic approach based on Collaborative Social Design-based research (Anderson & Shattuck, 2012). I first used a logbook to document the participants' social representations on linguistic and cultural diversity. I was taking notes and reflecting on the following: phone calls and email exchanges I had with the organizers (their requests or concerns regarding my intervention); the type of questions or concerns emerging during the workshops and informal exchanges during lunch time, breaks and post-workshops that I had with participants. Second, I reviewed post-workshop surveys conducted by the Ministry of Education. These surveys retraced the opinions of the participants about the workshops (strength and challenges for their practice). And, as a last source of data, I used the emails received from some teachers weeks after the workshops who voluntarily shared with me how they implemented the approach and the results of this implementation. The following section outlines the content of the workshops given for the Ministry of Education, after which, some results of the workshops will be discussed, based on the data collected.

Framing the Workshops on the Major Challenges of the French School System in Ontario

Coming from France, having spent 10 years in a French province in Canada (Quebec) and as a new researcher in Ontario, I first decided to familiarize myself with the context. I conducted a vast literature review on the challenges of education within a minority context. It gave me a better idea of the complexity of the situation and enabled me to frame my workshops on three main challenges in this specific case:

a. Linguistic insecurity
b. Duality between English and French first and then with the languages of immigration
c. French sustainability in the higher education system

Researchers have well documented the struggle of pupils to learn a language of instruction in a minority context (Landry, Allard, & Deveau, 2010; Lasagabaster, 2018). In Ontario specifically, several factors seem to contribute to pupils' linguistic insecurity: they feel they lack opportunities to speak French in an English environment, they feel they are not exposed enough to the target language and, most of the time, they feel more at ease speaking the dominant language. Moreover, two major policies impact the linguistic and cultural landscape of French-language school in Ontario today. First, article 23 of the Canadian Charter of Rights and Freedoms framed the access to French school. It is an access by parental right, meaning that, at least, one of a student's parents must have attended a French school in Canada. In many cases, pupils do not speak French at home but can be enrolled in a French school because of this policy. Second, with the increase of immigration, more and more pupils from a francophone background or not (allophone pupils) are now accepted in the French school system. The programme Memorandum 148 (Minister of Education, 2009[3]) allows for these pupils to gain access to French-language schools, as well as children who have grandparents who attended French-language schools in Canada. Classes are evidently extremely heterogeneous and teachers have the difficult role of purveying academic content anchored in a monolingual curriculum made for French speakers to a very linguistically and ethnically diverse population. In a minority context, teachers and school directors further feel that their mission is to protect French language and culture (Leurebourg, 2013). Thus, English and languages from pupils' repertoires are often denied by the school system to only promote French language and culture (Farmer, 2008; Fleuret et al., 2013). In addition, Lamoureux (2010) has highlighted the lack of French institutions at a secondary and university level that obviously impacts the sustainability of the French language and culture in Ontario.

These complex challenges formed the basis of my workshops and, because the literature is rich in this domain, I was able to base most of my content on empirical data. I tried to use each of the challenges as a starting point to nourish my workshop. For example, I presented the results of collaborative research conducted in Montreal (Armand, Lory, & Rousseau, 2013) with immigrant pupils in French schools participating in a Drama-based plurilingual project (inspired by "l'éveil aux langues") where pupils gained more confidence in speaking French and were more willing to speak French when other languages were not prohibited. I used this specific research in order to highlight how teachers, in their practices, could work collaboratively with pupils to try to overcome pupils' feeling of linguistic insecurity (a). To attend the duality between French and English, I then explained how instead of focusing on "false friends" between the two languages, we could use cognates as a linguistic strategy to develop better skills in French. The Montreal éveil aux langues project (www.elodil.umontreal.ca) offered learning video clips and activities in French on cognates that helped me to show how, in practice, it is possible to leverage pupils' abilities in English to support French language development. Multilingual children's literature abounds, and I presented a few bi/plurilingual books where French and other languages are used side by side (b). My last focal point concerned the sustainability of French language and culture in the province using Lamoureux's research (2010), which focuses on the problems pupils encounter when confronted with instruction in French at secondary and university level. Lamoureux concludes that it is the role of French teachers in Ontario, i.e. a plurilingual context in which French is a minority language, to support the desire and pleasure of speaking French (c). I used, again, different authentic materials (children literature, videos) and pedagogical material using plurilingual approaches to demonstrate how, in practice, it is possible to develop pleasure in learning French by using other languages. Finally, I demonstrated how Ontario's programmes support an inclusive pedagogical approach in order to legitimate such approaches in their practice. To sum up, I designed professional development workshops with the following strategies in mind: 1) to study the context and understand as well as possible the reality and challenges experienced by the customer; 2) to use these challenges as a starting point for a discussion and a reflexion supported by empirical data; 3) to explicitly show, in practice through video and with pedagogical materials, how a change is indeed possible and required; and, lastly, 4) I legitimized this change by highlighting the different Ministry of Education policies that, in fact, support such a plurilingual paradigm.

Consultancy and Acceptance

Considering the Impact of Social Representations in the Act of Teaching to Move from a Monolingual Paradigm to a Plurilingual Paradigm

The social psychology theory of Social Representation (Jodelet, 1989) informs us on the major impact of social ideologies on group behaviour. To deconstruct the social representations of educators on plurilingualism is a long-term process and requires reflection and questioning. The theory of Social Representation has been used as the basis for my advice to move from a monolingual paradigm to a plurilingual paradigm. In fact, it helped me convince the stakeholders of the value of the approach and the necessity of the workshops in order to support a long-term change. At different stages of the workshops, I invited the participants to share their experiences as learners, as teachers and as citizens of the world, highlighting the current multicultural and plurilingual reality. These spaces of discussion allowed participants to share their experiences on linguistic and cultural diversity and rethink their role as teachers/educators in the 21st century: nowadays, the responsibility of being a teacher extends beyond being the provider of school content to supporting pupils drawing on all of their linguistic and cultural experiences and knowledge in order to learn.

Creating/Supporting a Community of Practice

Changing practices requires motivation and support. Thus, I invited school boards' pedagogical consultants to support the teachers during the implementation/adaptation of the Awakening to languages programme, and I made myself available to work with the pedagogical counselors. The collaboration between teachers and pedagogical counselors remains one of the main success factors in the implementation of such a programme. By their presence in the schools, the pedagogical counselors were able to advise the teachers on how to implement and adjust the programme in a specific context and were able to document some successful practices. These practices were then communicated through social media to the community of practice. In my work with pedagogical counselors, I acted as mediator, linking theory and practice and discussing the challenges encountered in classrooms. With one of the school boards, we decided to write an article in a professional journal, extending our collaboration and reflecting on the benefits of such a partnership.

Final Reflection

The workshops indicated that participants who experienced living in cultural and linguistic diversity in their personal lives were more likely to embrace a plurilingual paradigm in their pedagogical practices. Moreover, when teachers were able to corroborate the data to their own experience, they were more responsive and willing to implement such a practice. Overall, teachers, school boards' pedagogical consultants and school directors were engaged in the process of changing their practices to respond more appropriately to the profile of their pupils. Although some participants considered formal pedagogical approaches like Awakening to languages pedagogy to be a drastic change, they expressed a keen interest in making an effort to welcome their pupils' linguistic and cultural background in the classroom.

The survey conducted by the Ministry of Education after the workshops also showed that participants were greatly interested in these innovative and inclusive approaches. The survey highlighted that many teachers felt overwhelmed by the situation and did not have enough resources to proceed. I received a few emails from participants, and I met teachers who had attended the workshops, saying they now applied a plurilingual and pluricultural approach in their teaching practice. They were eager to share their experiences and stressed the positive social impact of such practices on their pupils and on their relationship with them. For example, one teacher showed me pictures of plurilingual vocabulary maps that she created in her classroom with the collaboration of the entire class. She explained to me that now, when learning new vocabulary, pupils are trying to link these new words with some languages from the class linguistic repertoire. Changing teachers', school boards' pedagogical consultants' and school directors' social representations is a long-term process. I believe that these workshops are a stepping stone to a larger process that should include policy changes and more collaboration in the classroom. The pluricultural and plurilingual features of today's classroom require that educators rethink their role in order to better support their pupils. This case study suggests that shifting from traditional monolingual practices to more innovative and inclusive pedagogical practices that support linguistic and cultural diversity is a holistic process that requires the involvement and collaboration of all educators: teachers, their school boards' pedagogical consultants, school directors, the Ministry of Education, as well as researchers. This change is imperative if the curriculum is to present even more explicitly the benefits of the plurilingual and pluricultural classrooms of the 21st century.

Notes

1. http://laws-lois.justice.gc.ca/fra/Const/page-15.html
2. Program No 148, Ministry of Education of Ontario (2009)
3. www.edu.gov.on.ca/extra/eng/ppm/148.html

References

Anderson, T., & Shattuck, J. (2012). Design-based research: A decade of progress in education research? *Educational Researcher, 41*(1), 16–25.

Armand, F., Dagenais, D., & Nicollin, L. (2008). La dimension linguistique des enjeux interculturels: de l'Éveil aux langues à l'éducation plurilingue. In M. Mc Andrew (Ed.), *Rapport ethniques et éducation: perspectives nationale et internationale. Revue Éducation et Francophonie, XXXVI*(1), 44–64.

Armand, F., Lory, M.-P., & Rousseau, C. (2013). Les histoires, ça montre les personnes dedans, les feelings: Pas possible si pas de théâtre (Tahina). *Revue de linguistique et de didactique des langues, 48*, 37–55.

Blommaert, J., Collins, J., & Slembrouck, S. (2005). Spaces of multilingualism. *Language & Communication, 25*(3), 197–206.

Candelier, M. (2003). *L'éveil aux langues à l'école primaire. Evlang: bilan d'une innovation européenne*. Bruxelles: De Boeck.

Candelier, M., Camilleri-Grima, A., Castellotti, V., de Pietro, J.-F., Lőrincz, I., Meißner, F.-J., Noguerol, A. & Schröder-Sura, A. (2012). Le CARAP — Compétences et ressources. Strasbourg, France: Conseil de l'Europe. Retrieved from https://www.ecml.at/Resources/ECMLresources/tabid/277/ID/20/language/fr-FR/Default.aspx

Cavanagh, M., Cammarata, L., & Blain, S. (2016). Enseigner en milieu francophone minoritaire canadien: synthèse des connaissances sur les défis et leurs implications pour la formation des enseignants. *Canadian Journal of Education, 39*(4), 1–32.

Cummins, J. (2001). *Negotiating identities: Education for empowerment in a diverse society*. Los Angeles, CA: California Association for Bilingual Education.

Cummins, J. (2007). Rethinking monolingual instructional strategies in multilingual classrooms. *Canadian Journal of Applied Linguistics [Revue canadienne de linguistique appliquée], 10*(2), 221–240.

Farmer, D. (2008). Ma mère est de Russie, mon père est du Rwanda: Les familles immigrantes et leurs rapports à l'école en contexte francophone minoritaire. *Diversité Canadienne*, 124–127.

Fleuret, C., Bangou, F., & Ibrahim, A. (2013). Langues et enjeux interculturels: une exploration au coeur d'un programme d'appui à l'apprentissage du français de scolarisation pour les nouveaux arrivants. *Canadian Journal of Education, 36*(4), 280–298.

Flores, N., & Rosa, J. (2015). Undoing appropriateness: Raciolinguistic ideologies and language diversity in education. *Harvard Educational Review, 85*(2), 149–171.

Gérin-Lajoie, D. (2008). Le rôle contradictoire de l'école dans la construction des identités plurilingues. *Éducation et sociétés plurilingues*, *24*, 27–39.

Gogolin, I. (1994). *Der monolinguale Habitus der multilingualen Schule*. Münster: Waxmann-Verlag.

Jodelet, D. (1989). Représentations sociales: un domaine en expansion. In D. Jodelet (Ed.), *Les representations sociales* (pp. 47–78). Paris: Presses universitaires de France.

Lamoureux, S. (2010). L'aménagement linguistique en milieu scolaire francophone minoritaire en Ontario et l'accès aux études postsecondaires: interprétations et retombées. *Cahiers de l'ILOB*, *1*, 1–23.

Landry, R., Allard, R., & Deveau, K. (2010). *École et autonomie culturelle: enquête pancanadienne en milieu scolaire francophone minoritaire. Nouvelles perspectives canadiennes*. Rapport de recherche, Patrimoine Canada, Gatineau, et Institut canadien de recherche sur les minorités linguistiques, Moncton.

Lasagabaster, D. (2018). Language awareness in minority language contexts. In P. Garrett & J. M. Cots (Eds.), *The Routledge handbook of language awareness* (pp. 402–417). Abingdon, Oxon and New York, NY: Routledge.

Leurebourg, R. (2013). Rôles des directions d'école de langue française en situation minoritaire. *Canadian Journal of Education*, *36*(3), 272–297.

Lory, M.-P., & Armand, F. (2016). Éveil aux langues et évolution des représentations d'élèves plurilingues sur leur répertoire linguistique. *Alterstice*, *6*(1), 27–38.

Ministry of Education (2009). Program Memorandum No. 148. Policies Governing Admission to French-Language Schools in Ontario. Toronto, Ministry. Retrieved from http://www.edu.gov.on.ca/extra/eng/ppm/148.html

Prasad, G. (2012). Multiple minorities or plurilingual learners? Allophone immigrant children's rights and inclusion in French-language schools in Ontario. *Canadian Modern Language Review*, *68*(2), 190–215.

Statistique Canada. (2017). *Census 2016: Les enfants issus de l'immigration: un pont entre les cultures*. Retrieved from http://www12.statcan.gc.ca/census-recensement/2016/as-sa/98-200-x/2016015/98-200-x2016015-fra.cfm

Svalberg, A. (2009). Language awareness research: Where we are now. *Language Awareness*, *25*(1–2), 4–16.

Part IV
Non-Profit Organizations

Case Study 10

Improving Specialized Mental Healthcare and Social Services for Deaf and Hard of Hearing Newcomers

Anne Berghuis

The Case

In April 2015, I was asked by the director of the Mental Healthcare and Social Services organization (hence: the MHSS) for the deaf and hard of hearing in the Netherlands to research an urgent question and write an advisory report for the organization. The question was: "How can we, as an organization, build a better relationship with other organizations that, like us, come into contact with deaf and hard of hearing refugees in the Netherlands?" This question was motivated by the desire to improve specialized mental healthcare and social services for this very vulnerable target group from the very beginning of their stay in the Netherlands. The biggest obstacle to providing this immediate, initial care was the fact that refugees with a hearing impairment are untraceable in any Dutch system, as medical information is confidential. The MHSS for the deaf and hard of hearing is therefore often confronted with deaf former refugees that have lived in isolation for a very long time and found the needed specialized care only after many, often traumatic, years. Not only did this research have high social relevance, it also touched on both a highly topical socio-political issue and a twofold dimension of interculturality which became apparent during the research.

Why This Question?

Since 2013 the number of refugees seeking asylum in the Netherlands has increased, mainly due to the ongoing war in Syria (Vluchtelingenwerk Nederland, 2015). This phenomenon raised questions and posed challenges for decision makers in politics, education, healthcare and society as a whole. When refugees enter the Netherlands and apply for asylum, they have to go to the Immigration and Naturalisation Service (hence: INS) and take a number of steps to gain a temporary visa. When an asylum seeker is granted asylum, he or she will receive a temporary residence permit which is valid for five years (Asylum, n.d.). For hearing refugees, this multistep application is already quite overwhelming, let alone for deaf or hard of hearing refugees, as will be explained below.

First, for a deaf refugee it can be very hard to find and understand information, communicate, read forms and fill in documents (even with the help of an interpreter). This is mainly because there are great differences among countries and cultures as to the way deaf inhabitants are treated, including the educational opportunities they are offered. The language skills of a deaf refugee are therefore highly dependent on the educational opportunities he or she had in the country of origin. Second, the language barrier can be high. Each country has its own sign language and deaf people who lived in isolation may have developed their own so-called home signs. The combination of these factors makes it very challenging for the deaf refugee to feel safe, recover, integrate and socialize in the new country of residence. Also, the application process for deaf asylum seekers often takes much longer than nine months (Buytendijk, Batavier, & Van Rooij, 2015), which is the prolonged standard trajectory.

The MHSS for the deaf and hard of hearing wants to improve the experience and integration of deaf and hard of hearing refugees by organizing a clear and waterproof information and communication network between organizations that encounter deaf refugees. This way, information becomes accessible and no deaf refugee will go unnoticed, be excluded or forgotten. There are several obstacles, however, for both the refugees and services like the MHSS for the deaf and hard of hearing. These obstacles prevent the MHSS for the deaf and hard of hearing from providing the specialized and professional care to this vulnerable minority group.

The Organization

The MHSS for the deaf and hard of hearing is specialized in aiding deaf and hard of hearing people. The mission of the organization is: "aiding the deaf and hard of hearing to live the healthiest and most independent life possible, in order for them to be able to fully and actively participate in society" (GGMD voor Doven en Slechthorenden, 2016). In terms of concrete, practical aid, this can translate into, for example, employment advice, communication training, ambulatory therapy and much more. The MHSS for the deaf and hard of hearing is located in thirteen different cities in the Netherlands (Locaties en Aanbod, n.d.) and employs around 150 professionals, including psychiatrists, psychologists, psycho-motorial therapists, communication specialists, interpreters, ambulatory nurses, social workers, sign language teachers and many others (Functies binnen GGMD, n.d.). These all meet with their own clients, but because one client can be provided with support by multiple professionals, all professionals meet in a multidisciplinary meeting each week to discuss the treatment plan, progress of the client or completion of care.

The MHSS for the deaf and hard of hearing must abide by the healthcare norms and rules of the government and is very much dependent on government support for funding. As a non-profit healthcare foundation, the care and services it provides are mostly paid for by the clients' health insurances. In times of cuts and reorganization of health insurance policies, mental healthcare and social services organizations in general are struggling. The MHSS has to safeguard the quality of its care and account to the government, the client, management and other stakeholders (GGMD voor Doven en Slechthorenden, 2013). Its dependence on government funding and on invoicing health insurance companies can complicate providing care to refugees and asylum seekers without an official residence permit, because without such a permit, an asylum seeker cannot apply for health insurance.

Intercultural Dimensions

This case study has an interesting twofold intercultural dimension. Not only do Dutch culture and the refugee's national culture meet, deaf people also know their own culture, deaf culture, which is not bound to a specific place. It has been reported that deaf people often feel part of the same community as they share their way of communicating and experiencing the hearing world around them. They like to interact, because they identify with each other and have no problems expressing a feeling of mutual understanding. Therefore, they may be more inclined to see themselves as a cultural minority in the hearing world and do not identify with the target group of disabled people, which is how hearing people often see them. In this way, deaf people live in two cultures: the deaf and the hearing culture. This adds the second intercultural dimension to this research topic. Given the multiple dimensions, this research fits into the discipline of intercultural communication in a unique way.

The Research Process

Brainstorming Session

I gladly accepted the challenge of taking on this research question and sat down with the director and a deaf volunteer who counselled deaf refugee couples for a brainstorming session. I used this meeting not so much to devise the research method, but to get a clearer picture of the questions, obstacles and ideas in the minds of the director and stakeholders. It was during this meeting that I suggested the formulation of the main research question as stated previously. I believe the brainstorming session was very important for multiple reasons: 1) the organization felt heard and trusted me to shape the research as I thought suitable; 2) I got to know the organizational structure and its values, with which both the research and advisory report had to be compatible; and 3) I obtained information on actions the organization had already undertaken to solve this issue. In other words, as a researcher I identified the gap my research (partly) needed to fill. We agreed to maintain contact about my activities and research.

Earlier Research, Choosing the Research Method and Respondents

I knew I was not goin to interview deaf refugees. There was a ten-week deadline and one of the obstacles was that deaf refugees were very hard to find in the first place. Tracking them would take up too much time. Moreover, if I were to find deaf refugees, the interviews would be contingent on their willingness to be interviewed, their emotional and physical condition and their language skills. Buytendijk et al. (2015) had outlined the needs of deaf refugees and I wanted to find out how the MHSS for the deaf and hard of hearing could become involved in answering these needs by working together with other organizations.

To answer the organization's question, I first had to establish how the needs of deaf refugees could best be met. With this information the MHSS for the deaf and hard of hearing would be able to identify the organizations and people with which to work and build a better relationship. I consulted the director and my fellow communication colleagues to make a list of experts within their network who would be willing to talk to me. I then discussed my progress with the MHSS for the deaf and hard of hearing and we decided that qualitative research by means of conducting semi-structured expert interviews based on a topic list was the best method to use. A semi-structured interview would enable me to bring up a set of topics of my choice but would also provide room for the expert to bring additional, valuable information to the interview. There is a great deal of knowledge about this topic, but it is shared among a small group of people. On top of that, the issue at stake was a big and complex one. In the end, the expert interviews would allow us to find out how deaf experts thought about care for deaf refugees and possible future cooperation with the MHSS for the deaf and hard of hearing, how well the MHSS for the deaf and hard of hearing was known and how these experts envisioned creating a shared network or protocol.

The Interviews

After reading into the methodology and the research theme further, I started contacting experts, scheduling interviews and developing questions. One research article provided clear guidance to create a tripartite topic list for the interview. Ward, Amas, and Lagnado (2008) wrote an extensive report on disabled refugees and asylum seekers in Great Britain, addressing themes like communication, culture and facilities. These three themes became the main themes for my interviews, as they touched on both the director's question and intercultural communication. I formulated relevant questions and made an interview planning according to Luo and Wildemuth (2009). I formulated the main question and the three thematic sub-questions directed at the experts as follows:

- MQ: How can existing challenges in dealing with deaf and hard of hearing refugees be handled in the best way possible?
- SQ1: What are the challenges and their solutions when it comes to communication with deaf and hard of hearing refugees?
- SQ2: What role does culture play in dealing with deaf and hard of hearing refugees?
- SQ3: What do deaf and hard of hearing refugees specifically need when they arrive in the Netherlands?

These questions and their ramifications were discussed in the structured form of the interview. In the open part of the interview I probed: "Is there anything else I forgot to ask or that we did not discuss that you would like to add or underline?"

I scheduled eleven interviews over the next couple of weeks and reserved an hour for each interview, considering interpreting time with the deaf experts. I interviewed six deaf experts, among them an ambulatory nurse, the volunteer I met during the brainstorming session, a Dutch sign language teacher/head social worker in a psychiatric facility, a Dutch sign language teacher/communication trainer and two deaf entrepreneurs who travelled and met other deaf people all around the world. Among the hearing experts were a lector of deaf studies, a legal interpreter, a social worker/coordinator client intake, a former director of a nursing home for deaf elderly people and a social worker/case manager. I received permission to record each interview and transcribed them afterwards in the office.

Analysis

To analyse the results, I started highlighting the valuable information thematically. I gathered interesting new insights and practical ideas, summarized them and categorized them under the themes communication, culture or facilities. Sometimes it was hard to divide information by theme as insights often touched on multiple themes, e.g. both communication and culture, or both culture and facilities. Some insights and ideas were mentioned by multiple different experts, in which case I summarized the information and marked it as a frequently mentioned solution or insight.

Consultancy and Acceptance

The next step was to write the actual advisory report and convert the obtained information, ideas, insights, suggestions and solutions into clear steps that the MHSS for the deaf and hard of hearing could undertake next. The two most frequently suggested steps by the experts were:

1. To create a communication platform where deaf specialists in politics, healthcare and education could share knowledge and information or make requests for referring deaf refugees to each other's services. On the one hand, organizations are often unknowingly inept when it comes to dealing with deafness. On the other hand, organizations specialized in working for and with deaf and hard of hearing people are often ignorant of the more complex legislation when it comes to immigration and integration of refugees. All experts pointed out their willingness to actively participate in such a platform.
2. To organize an asylum seekers centre with a specialized "deaf or hard of hearing refugee" department situated in the heart of the Netherlands and near a location of the MHSS for the deaf and hard of hearing. This would be much more efficient when it comes to deploying social workers and interpreters. This would also mean that the required facilities would always be ready when deaf refugees arrive at the centre.

These suggestions could be taken up by the MHSS for the deaf and hard of hearing. My personal further advice to the MHSS organization was to:

1. Approach this issue by working in or with a multidisciplinary team of people. Using the willingness of the experts to work together and make a joint effort to stay in touch is a great way to start the information and communication flow.
2. Document current activities within the organization regarding deaf and hard of hearing refugees and document future co-working activities in the previously mentioned multidisciplinary team/network. The documentation serves the purpose of learning from previous mistakes or

successes and of making information available and accessible to stake-holders. In addition, I strongly advised the MHSS to keep stakehold-ers updated on the organization's activities regarding the issue, to keep stakeholders informed and involved.

3. Appoint a refugee specialist within the organization. The MHSS for the deaf and hard of hearing has multiple self-made specialists when it comes to hearing loss or the deaf-blind. One of the experts advised appointing and training such a specialist for deaf and hard of hearing refugees. This would be much cheaper and more efficient than hiring someone for the job. This new specialist could also be the liaison between the MHSS for the deaf and hard of hearing and other organizations.

Final Reflection

My advisory report was received well and a few weeks later the management team discussed the report in a meeting. I received an e-mail with their points of action:

- We are contacting a group of legal interpreters to see if they can provide access to their contacts within the INS.
- A volunteer (the same volunteer who was present during the first brain-storm session) is busy contacting asylum seekers centres to stress the importance of alerting the MHSS for the deaf and hard of hearing when a new deaf or hard of hearing refugee is localized.
- We are currently trying to reach deaf and hard of hearing refugees living in the 390 municipalities in the Netherlands through **Stichting Vluchte-lingenwerk** (the Dutch Council for Refugees).
- Our contract manager is making a detailed calculation of the costs.
- The department of development made plans to provide a number of courses for refugees (ICT training, language training, etc.).
- We are deciding which recommendations are to be taken up by the MHSS for the deaf and hard of hearing and which recommendations and action points will be passed on to external organizations for further action.

References

Asylum. (n.d.). *Immigration and naturalisation service*. Retrieved from https://ind.nl/EN/asylum/pages/permanent-asylum-residence-permit.aspx

Buytendijk, E., Batavier, K., & Van Rooij, S. (2015). *Problemen die Dove Asiel-zoekers Ervaren bij een Asielaanvraag in Nederland* (Unpublished master thesis). Retrieved from www.dovenschap.nl/rapport-dove-asielzoekers/

Functies binnen GGMD. (n.d.). *GGMD voor Doven en Slechthorenden.* Retrieved from www.ggmd.nl/over-ggmd/deskundige-medewerkers/functies-binnen-ggmd/

GGMD voor Doven en Slechthorenden. (2013). *Professioneel Statuut GGMD voor Doven en Slechthorenden.* Gouda [PDF].

GGMD voor Doven en Slechthorenden. (2016). *Missie GGMD.* Gouda [PDF].

Locaties en Aanbod. (n.d.). Retrieved from www.ggmd.nl/contact/locaties-en-aanbod/

Luo, L., & Wildemuth, B. M. (2009). Semistructured interviews. In B. M. Wildemuth (Ed.), *Applications of social research methods to questions in information and library science* (1st ed., pp. 232–241). Westport: Libraries Unlimited.

VluchtelingenWerk Nederland. (2015). *Vluchtelingen in Getallen* [Data file]. Retrieved from www.vluchtelingenwerk.nl/sites/public/u895/Vluchtelingeninget allen2016.pdf

Ward, K., Amas, N., & Lagnado, J. (2008). *Supporting disabled refugees and asylum seekers: Opportunities for new approaches.* Retrieved from http://equality-ne.co.uk/downloads/336_Supportingdisabledrefugeesandasylumseekers.pdf

Case Study 11

A Model Village Constitution for Indigenous Traditional Leaders in Suriname

Ellen-Rose Kambel and Caroline de Jong

The Case

The Lower-Marowijne Area, the location of this case study, is situated in the northeastern tip of Suriname, a former Dutch colony which achieved independence in 1975. The Marowijne River to the east and the Atlantic Ocean to the north form its natural boundaries. This area has been occupied and used by eight indigenous communities for as long as they can remember. These communities are of the Kari'na (Carib) and Lokono (Arowak) indigenous cultures: five Kari'na villages: Christiaankondre, Langamankondre, Erowarte, Tapuku and Pierrekondre and three Lokono villages: Marijkedorp, Alfonsdorp and Bigi Ston. The total population of these communities is approximately 2,000. It is claimed that there used to be significant linguistic and cultural differences between the Kari'na and Lokono. However today there seem to be more socio-economic and even linguistic similarities than there are distinctions. In all the communities, most people speak Sranan (Sranan Tongo, which is also the vernacular). Most also have a reasonable understanding of Dutch, the country's official language. Only in two villages is the indigenous language spoken widely among young and old (Kari'na in Christiaankondre and Langamankondre, see Berghuis, 2016; Le Pichon & Kambel, 2016). There are few opportunities for formal education and community members typically make a living from subsistence and commercial fishing, shifting cultivation, hunting and low-wage informal employment. The area is noted for its high biological and cultural diversity and encompasses two nature reserves, the Wanekreek Nature Reserve and Galibi Nature Reserve. It also contains important archeological sites (see for a detailed description: Kambel & De Jong, 2006).

The Clients

In 2003, the Lower-Marowijne communities formed the Organization of Kari'na and Lokono in Marowijne (or KLIM) as a regional umbrella organization. The communities are represented through their traditional governments (village councils) which consist of a village chief (or *kapitein*) and two or three assistants (*basyas*). The chiefs and *basyas* are the members of KLIM. At the time of the request, the KLIM had a full-time coordinator and a small local office where village members had access to a computer, a printer, internet and a small library.

The chiefs are also members of the national association of indigenous village leaders in Suriname (VIDS), which is headquartered in the capital city Paramaribo and about a three-hour drive away from the KLIM territory. The VIDS was established in 1992 to further the interests of the traditional authorities of the indigenous peoples in Suriname who represent about 5% of the total population. Despite having the oldest traditional governing system of Suriname, the indigenous chiefs and village councils and their customary rules for governing their communities have never been legally recognized by the central government (see Kambel & MacKay, 2003). Strengthening the indigenous traditional governments and gaining recognition of their rights to the lands they have traditionally occupied and used have been priorities of both the VIDS and the KLIM since their inception.

Land Rights

Since the European colonization of Suriname in 1650, all lands in Suriname have been considered State lands. Only those with a land title, i.e. proof of land ownership in the form of a written document issued by the colonial government, were able to legally claim that they had rights to the land (Kambel & MacKay, 2003). The indigenous peoples who had no such titles, but who had collectively used the forest, rivers and creeks for hundreds of years, were not only excluded from the protection of their property, but could also only gain protection if they were willing to accept a form of individual ownership. Since 1996, discussions have taken place in villages across Suriname, facilitated by the VIDS, about the communities' preference: individual or collective land rights. The KLIM communities were the first in Suriname to opt for collective land rights. They were also the first to map their territory (in 2000) and to start a legal case against the government to secure recognition and protection of land rights. In 2007, a formal complaint was filed with the Inter-American Commission on Human Rights. In November 2015, almost eight years later, the Inter-American Court of Human Rights, the highest judicial body in the Organization of American States (OAS), found that Suriname had violated the human rights of the Lower-Marowijne indigenous peoples and ordered the State to legally recognize and protect their collective lands and resources.[1]

The Question

In 2006, the KLIM requested technical assistance to develop a land management plan (LMP). There were several reasons why the village leaders wanted a LMP. First of all, it was considered part of their long-term aim for self-governance and sustainable development of their territory. During a previous project the authors had been involved in, to document the traditional use of their territory, it had become apparent that some parts of the territory were already under pressure as a result of logging and mining activities, but also because of overuse by their own community members. The KLIM communities were also warned that once their land rights were legally recognized, this would not signal the end of the struggle. On the contrary, examples from Indonesia, among others, had shown that communities could easily be persuaded to rent out their lands for uncontrolled timber cutting. Second, the eight communities of the Lower-Marowijne had informally agreed traditional boundaries, indicating where the territory of one village started and the other ended, but they also used a large part of the territory communally. To prevent future conflicts, it was agreed that a land management plan would be necessary. Finally, having a land management plan in place was considered strategically important to support the KLIM court case as the KLIM could thus demonstrate that they had advanced plans in place to conserve and manage the territory well.

The authors were asked to facilitate this process. Ellen-Rose Kambel, a Surinamese-Dutch lawyer, had worked with the communities since 1997, when she started her PhD research on gender and indigenous rights and had continued to facilitate workshops on indigenous rights and to provide legal technical assistance to the KLIM communities. Caroline de Jong, a Dutch historian, had also previously worked with the communities to assist with a historical documentation project in 2004 in support of the communities' legal case. In 2005, we worked together in the same area on the previously mentioned project to document traditional use of natural resources. This was done in the form of a community-based research project, for which we had trained community members to collect information and document the traditional ways that the communities use their territory.[2] As with that project, the VIDS served as the official project holder and the project was funded by the Rainforest Foundation-US. We were both hired as consultants by the VIDS through an agreement with the UK-based non-governmental organization Forest Peoples Programme (FPP).

The Research Process

We decided that a SWOT (Strengths, Weaknesses, Opportunities and Threats) analysis would be a useful tool to gain a clearer picture of the long-term vision of the communities: what sort of community would they like to have in 20 or 50 years and what implications does that have for the natural resources they traditionally use? In August 2006, we organized a planning workshop with the KLIM. We started out with presenting the results of a longitudinal study of economically successful indigenous nations in North America (Cornell, Jorgensen, Kalt, & Spilde, 2005). This study found that economic success for indigenous nations depended on four factors:

1. Self-rule: meaning that indigenous peoples must be able to have decision making power and not be dependent on governments or non-governmental organizations and donors;
2. Good governance: it was shown that self-rule alone was not enough, there must be capable governing institutions in place, free from nepotism and corruption;
3. Cultural match: the governance institutions must fit indigenous conceptions of how authority should be organized and exercised. So instead of introducing new governing institutions (such as a western style parliamentary democracy), successful North American indigenous nations had strengthened their own traditional governing systems, which are often based on consensus and the authority of elders; and
4. Strategic orientation: the nations concerned had considered the kind of society they wished to build in the long term and which decisions they needed to make now and had subsequently followed through on their vision.

Our original idea was that the SWOT analysis in Lower-Marowijne would focus on developing the strategic orientation (factor 4). We had prepared for training community researchers in doing SWOT analyses in all eight communities. However, after we presented the previously mentioned study to the village leaders, they picked up on factor (2) and decided that they first needed to strengthen their traditional governance systems. They argued that in order for the village councils to guide their communities toward a 'strategic orientation', they should have an effective village government. This change in programme focus affected the budget and time line, so we sought and gained approval from our funder, the Rainforest Foundation-US.

Research Activities

The next day, we started a four-day training session with the eight community members (one from each village) who had originally been selected for the SWOT analysis. During the training, which focused mainly on research techniques, the researchers developed a participatory action-oriented study.

A first aim of the research, which was decided on together with the community researchers, was to first analyse the problems regarding traditional government and then, together with the community members and the village leaders, the goal was to come up with practical solutions and strategies for improving the traditional leadership and government of the eight villages. First, a household questionnaire was developed for two purposes: (1) to share information about the project: each household would be visited and would be provided with an explanation of the project and (2) to assess the community's opinions about the village council. This consisted mainly of questions about communication, as communication was perceived to be an important bottleneck according to both the village leaders and the community researchers. In total 350 persons, or 17% of the total population, were interviewed. Further, semi-structured individual interviews were held with 35 Elders. These interviews were conducted to gain information about the way the villages were governed in the past and to learn from the strengths and weaknesses of the traditional government system in the past. Finally, the researchers conducted group interviews in each community using the SWOT methodology, but instead of focusing on the long-term vision as originally planned, this SWOT was about the village government systems. The fieldwork took place between August and November 2006. In late November 2006, we returned briefly to evaluate the project activities with the coordinator and the community researchers. The researchers all indicated that they found the study extremely interesting and important and that they had received positive feedback from the village members.

Consultancy and Acceptance

Action Plan for Strengthening the Village Councils

In February 2007, a first draft report of the study was discussed with the researchers and the results were cross-checked. After this, a three-day workshop was held to discuss the outcome with the members of the KLIM. During this workshop, the village leaders and *basyas* also performed a Strengths, Weaknesses, Opportunities and Threats analysis of their own traditional government. Interestingly, many of their findings corresponded with the outcome of the 'people SWOT', indicating a strong basis for consensus. On the second and third day of the workshop, the council members broke up into working groups and developed an Action Plan for Strengthening the Village Councils, using the results of the study and the recommendations that were suggested by the people.

One of the main outcomes of the research was that it was unclear to the community members what exactly were the role, responsibilities and tasks

Ellen-Rose Kambel and Caroline de Jong

Figure 11.1 Village Leaders Discussing the Outcome of the Village Consultations
(2007)

of the village government. Also, there were many complaints about the communication between the village council and the community: the community members felt that there were not enough village meetings organized by the village councils; the council members were not adequately prepared and did not provide good quality information during the meetings; and decisions were taken without properly consulting with the community. On the other hand, there was also a lack of participation on the part of the community. As one community member said: "He [the chief] does his duty but the people don't show up. So, the people are to blame" (KLIM, 2007, p. 40).

It was recommended that a Model Village Constitution should be drafted. A village constitution would lend more legitimacy to a land management plan as it would be clear to everyone what the tasks and responsibilities were of the village traditional government. This had never before been written down and the village members had indicated that they needed such clarity.

After discussing the Action Plan with the communities in April 2007, a second round of consultations was held by the community leaders on their own. Because insufficient feedback resulted from these meetings, the KLIM decided that they themselves should not be present during this workshop. They felt that people would be more comfortable to speak in the absence of the village council. They suggested that community members should be trained to facilitate workshops on the Action Plan. In addition, each community elected two representatives who would be responsible for organizing a fourth round of discussion in their own village and who would attend a larger meeting to elaborate a first draft of a village constitution. In July 2007, the third round of community meetings was held, this time facilitated by the KLIM coordinator and two former KLIM researchers with assistance from the consultants. The way the workshops were set up was that the village leader would officially open the meeting and then leave, along with the village assistants. The project team then explained the purpose of the workshop and the group was divided into three break-out groups to discuss a section of the points in the Action Plan and comment on them. Each small group was facilitated by a project team member. Each of the three groups selected a rapporteur who presented the comments to the plenary. This method had the expected positive results: there was a lively general discussion and the people managed to agree on their comments to most points. Eventually, in May 2008, a Model Village Constitution was adopted by all eight villages. The Model Village Constitution of Lower-Marowijne is a basic text allowing variations on some issues, which were bracketed for this purpose. Each village decided what these variations would be. For example, the Model Village Constitution provided that all village councils are required to meet at least "[xx] number of times per year". Some villages decided that three times was sufficient, whereas others wanted their councils to meet at least four times a year.

Today, 10 years later, the Model is still used in the communities, especially for elections of the village councils, as it includes clear guidelines on how village council members should be elected or appointed (depending on the village's preference). The Model was also adopted in another area of Suriname (District of Para) and it is generally used as a guideline by the national organization VIDS for elections in all indigenous communities.

Final Reflection

To conclude this case study, we want to reflect on two issues: the role of interculturality and the fundamental principle underlying this case study, namely indigenous peoples' right to self-determination. The right to self-determination is a principle of international law pertaining to all peoples. Since the adoption of articles 3 and 4 of the United Nations Declaration on the Rights of Indigenous Peoples (adopted in 2007), it has also been explicitly extended to indigenous peoples:

Article 3. *Indigenous peoples have the right to self-determination. By virtue of that right they freely determine their political status and freely pursue their economic, social and cultural development.*

Article 4. *Indigenous peoples, in exercising their right to self-determination, have the right to autonomy or self-government in matters relating to their internal and local affairs, as well as ways and means for financing their autonomous functions.*

The same declaration, which was approved by Suriname, also provides in article 5 that "Indigenous peoples have the right to maintain and strengthen their distinct political, legal, economic, social and cultural institutions".

An integral element of the right to self-determination is the right of indigenous peoples to give or withhold their *free, prior and informed consent* (FPIC) over any decisions that affect their communities and their natural resources. Governments as well as private industries (e.g. mining or logging companies), but also nature conservation organizations wishing to establish nature protection regulations or reserves, must respect these rights, failure of which may lead to termination of the license to operate. Often, consultants are hired to engage with the indigenous peoples involved. Lack of knowledge about what constitutes effective participation or FPIC can have serious consequences for the indigenous communities (see for examples of FPIC processes: Colchester & Farhan Ferrari, 2007; Weitzner, 2011). In our case, the question to develop a land management plan and a village constitution was not an external one, but was suggested by the communities themselves as represented by the KLIM board. Still, as our discussion of the success factors following shows, the case study provides important lessons for students of intercultural communication who may find employment at consultancy firms, government or resource industries and who may be engaged in consultation processes with indigenous communities.

Interculturality

Interculturality issues arose at different levels: with regard to the content and with regard to the actors involved. Regarding *content*: land management plans were originally developed in and for industrialized, western contexts where written laws and regulations ensured compliance. In this case we were dealing with a rural setting and an indigenous territory where unwritten traditional laws govern the behaviour of the population, alongside formal national legislation. When it became clear that the village leaders wanted to strengthen their governance and that a written village constitution would be the outcome, this added another layer of interculturality. The question was how to reconcile the traditional rules which had developed over centuries, and which are characterized by flexibility and ability to adapt to various social changes, with a western concept of written laws of which the goal is to create legal certainty and which are therefore *intended* to be static even though in practice they are of course also flexibly used.[3] The Model Village Constitution constitutes an interesting hybrid because it provides some measure of legal certainty on the local level. We heard especially from *basyas* (the village assistants) that they were happy with the Village Constitution, because whenever they have a problem, either with their boss, the village chief or with a villager, they could show them what the rules were. On the other hand, the Surinamese national legislation is silent about the status of the indigenous traditional government. From a Surinamese legal perspective, the Model Constitution has no legitimacy and would probably not be upheld by a judge.[4] With regard to the *actors* involved: as mentioned earlier, the consultants had a Dutch/urban Surinamese background, and we spoke (with) different languages/accents than the clients. There was also a difference in formal education. Although the KLIM members and the community researchers differed culturally and linguistically from the consultants (and to some extent from each other, speaking different mother tongues and belonging to different communities), they were of course the experts with regard to the traditional governing system and the practice of government as experienced by them daily as members of the communities.

What Did Not Work

Parts of the draft Model Village Constitution were non-negotiable for the village leaders. They were clearly reluctant to give up some of their power. The village leaders would sometimes simply refuse to agree to accept any consequences if they themselves were to break the newly written down rules. When the community researchers and the especially elected and trained village representatives along with the consultants would insist that a solution was needed in case of conflicting views, the village leaders would simply say: "Don't worry. It is our tradition, so of course we will do it!" Eventually, during implementation, these particular provisions proved indeed to be so-called paper tigers lacking any teeth. For instance: it was agreed in the Village Constitution that village councils had to organize village meetings at least x number of times per year. However, in the case that no village meetings were organized, there was only the option that the head *basya* would call a meeting. If the head *basya* refused or did not want to come into conflict with his or her 'boss', there were no further repercussions. At least in one community, the village council did not call meetings for an extended period of time (over a year); in fact the village leader moved to the capital city, only returning once in a while. Despite the Village Constitution, the community has been unable to resolve the situation.

What Did Work

Still, the adoption of a Model Village Constitution and its use and implementation after 10 years should be viewed as the successful outcome of a long process to strengthen the local village governments. The reasons for its success, we speculate, are:

- a long-term engagement of the consultants with the communities, which meant that there was a high degree of mutual trust;
- one of the consultants' cultural background as Surinamese, her ability to communicate in Sranan and/or Surinamese Dutch. Conversely: almost all KLIM board members had spent time in the capital city, either in their youth or later during the interior conflict (1986–1992) when they had become internally displaced and had learned to speak either Dutch and/or Sranan fluently. This created considerable cultural and linguistic understanding between the consultants and the KLIM board members.
- a flexible donor: without the support of the Rainforest Foundation-US to allow for changes in the original project design, we would not have been able to make such drastic changes to the project and ensure that it conformed to what the communities wanted to achieve. While the project was planned for one year, it eventually took two years to complete. This time was clearly necessary to follow all the steps to ensure the full and effective participation of the communities at all levels.
- using an indigenous framework: we purposely looked for good examples from other indigenous peoples and employed the findings of the Harvard study which were based on economically successful North American indigenous nations. We also obtained advice from colleagues who were engaged in a similar process with indigenous peoples in neighbouring Guyana, who share many of the same cultural characteristics with the Surinamese indigenous people.
- the fact that researchers from the communities were carrying out the research and facilitating the meetings – working in the local language and underlining the ownership of the initiative of the communities themselves. The researchers were known and trusted and knew the specific cultural dos and don'ts that outsiders or the consultants themselves would not have, possibly resulting in other outcomes.

The most important success factor was, in our opinion, the fact that the leaders themselves had requested the study. They had wanted to strengthen their local government themselves. It was their own idea and they were personally involved in all the steps that were taken. In other words, through the project, the traditional leaders as representatives of their communities expressed and executed their right to self-determination.

Notes

1. Inter-American Court of Human Rights, Case of the Saramaka People v. Suriname, Judgment of November 28, 2007. Retrieved from www.corteidh.or.cr/docs/casos/articulos/seriec_172_ing.pdf
2. See: Kambel, E.-R., & De Jong, C. (Eds.). (2010). *Marauny Na'na Emandobo / Lokono Shikwabana ("Marowijne – our territory") – Traditional use and management of the Lower Marowijne area by the Kaliña and Lokono.* Retrieved from www.forestpeoples.org/topics/customary-sustainable-use/publication/2010/suri name-10c-case study
3. For example: legislation can be changed and are subject to interpretation by courts. Consider also the Dutch *gedoogbeleid* where authorities tolerate violation of laws for practical reasons (e.g. the softdrugs policy).
4. This should be tested in court and the indigenous communities may have a powerful argument from international human rights law which recognizes their right to self-determination, including their right to self-governance (see UN Declaration on the Rights of Indigenous Peoples, articles 3 and 4; Inter-American Human Rights Court, judgment in the Saramaka case 2007).

References

Berghuis, A. (2016). *Taalattitude onder de Inheemsen in Suriname: Een Onderzoek naar Taalkeuze, Taaldominantie en Taalpreferentie* (Unpublished master's thesis). Utrecht University, Utrecht, The Netherlands.

Colchester, M., & Farhan Ferrari, M. (2007). *Making FPIC work: Challenges and prospects for indigenous peoples.* Moreton-in-Marsh: Forest Peoples Programme.

Cornell, S., Jorgensen, M., Kalt, J., & Spilde, K. (2005). *Seizing the future: Why some native nations do and others don't* (Joint Occasional Papers on Native Affair No. 2005-01). Native Nations Institute University of Arizona and the Harvard Project on American Indian Economic Development.

Kambel, E.-R., & de Jong, C. (Eds.). (2006). *Marauny Na'Na Emandobo Lokono Shikwabana. 'Marowijne: Our Territory'.* Moreton-in-Marsh: Forest Peoples Programme. Retrieved from www.forestpeoples.org/documents/conservation/suriname_10c_feb06_dutch.pdf

Kambel, E.-R., & MacKay, F. (2003). *De rechten van inheemse volken en marrons in Suriname.* Leiden: KITLV Press.

KLIM. (2007). *Rapport Versterking van het Inheems Traditioneel Bestuur in Beneden-Marowijne.* Unpublished report, on file with authors.

Le Pichon, E., & Kambel, E-R. (2016). *Challenges of mathematics education in a multilingual post-colonial context: The case of Suriname.* Human rights in language and STEM education. Edited by Z. Babaci-Wilhite. Rotterdam: Sense Publishers, 221–240.

Weitzner, V. (2011). *Tipping the power balance. Making free, prior and informed consent work: Lessons & policy directions from 10 years of action research on extractives with indigenous and Afro-descendent peoples in the Americas.* Ottawa: The North-South Institute. Retrieved from www.nsi-ins.ca/wp-content/uploads/2012/10/2011-Tipping-the-Power-Balance-Making-Free-Prior-and-In formed-Consent-Work.pdf

Case Study 12

Photographers' Handling of Cultural Rituals and Conventions of Bereaved Parents After the Loss of a Child

Maaike Aans and Wieke Eefting[1]

The Case

In 2008 the non-governmental organization Make a Memory (hereafter: MaM) was founded in the Netherlands. This foundation offers free professional photoshoots to families with children who are terminally ill or who have lost a child. The children are between the age of 23 weeks of pregnancy to 17 years old. Most of the children who are photographed are babies who have passed away before, during or shortly after birth. The pictures that are taken during these photoshoots may be very valuable in the mourning process of the parents and other family members. In the 10 years of its existence, MaM has produced photo series of more than 8,000 children (and their relatives). The photo sessions are done by professional photographers. In order to guarantee high-quality photos MaM screens the photographers on their professionalism before letting them work for the foundation. Over 140 photographers (all of Dutch descent) covering the entire country are currently working for MaM. The photographers work on a voluntary basis and the photo sessions are completely free of cost for the parents. The parents receive a booklet with five printed pictures after the session and a USB stick with all the photos. The rights of the pictures belong to the parents, which means no one is allowed to spread or print these pictures without their permission. The foundation is solely dependent on gifts and donations, and the effort of its volunteers.

Families from all layers of the Dutch society are able to request a photoshoot. Just like many other parts of the world, Dutch society is increasingly diverse. This culturally diverse society is likewise reflected within the families the photographers working for MaM encounter during their work for the organization. Together with the cultural backgrounds of the families, different cultural and religious rituals and conventions concerning mourning become relevant in the work of MaM. In general, for parents with a western background, having pictures taken of their dead child is commonly accepted, while this is not always so for parents from other parts of the world. Additionally, the notion of saving face could have an impact on the photo session and the composition of the photos (Goffman, 1967). In order to communicate effectively and respectfully across cultures, one should not only show appropriate behaviour but also be able to handle the psychological demands and dynamic effects of those interactions. This ability is enhanced by developing intercultural interaction competences (Spencer-Oatey & Franklin, 2009).

One of the photographers working for MaM contacted the research group Intercultural Communication at Utrecht University because she and several colleagues experienced difficulties in understanding and working with the variety of cultural rituals and conventions. They noticed that these differences can affect their work as photographers in a negative way. Together with the Board of MaM a formal request for advice on how to deal with intercultural situations was addressed to the research group. Maaike Aans, then a master's student at Utrecht University, formulated the research question in close collaboration with two supervisors and a representative of the foundation. In addition, a consultancy question was formulated in order to provide advice to the foundation. After face-to-face meetings with a representative of the Board of MaM, the photographer involved and the supervisor of Intercultural Communication, phone calls and email contact, the research and consultancy questions were adjusted to the wishes of the organization until all parties were satisfied with the following questions.

Research Question

Which differences concerning death and mourning do the photographers of Make a Memory encounter during the photo sessions with families from diverse cultural backgrounds?

Consultancy Question

In what way can the photographers optimally handle their communication with, and anticipate on, the differences concerning death and mourning that they encounter during the photo sessions with families from diverse cultural backgrounds?

One of the supervisors, Wieke Eefting, is a photographer for the foundation herself, which made it easy for the researcher, Aans, to get input on core problems. Weekly discussions about the project ensured that the researcher was able to keep the client in mind and adjust the research during the project to wishes and preferences of the organization.

The Research Process

The research has been conducted using an iterative, qualitative research method. By means of 18 semi-structured, in-depth interviews with a research population characterized by triangulation, the researcher has been able to offer insights regarding the research question. The participants consisted of photographers, bereaved parents, medical experts, an imam and a priest. The researcher coded the transcripts of the interviews in order to distill the required information.

By using an institutional, ethnographic approach, the researcher was able to create an outline of the process of a MaM photo session. The outcome was visualized into a praxeogram, displaying the interconnections and actions occurring in the process of a photoshoot (DeVault & McCoy, 2001; Ehlich & Rehbein, 1972). A praxeogram is used to display the ruling relations and the way interconnections in an organizational process exist (ibid.). The praxeogram offers insights in the standardized actions that occur during the process of a MaM photo session, and the different points of decision that could influence these actions. The praxeogram is divided in different segments and phases. This way, different intercultural and institutional aspects that influence the process of a photo session are displayed (Figure 12.1).

Figure 12.1 shows that the actors involved are the parents, the caretaker, the photographer and MaM. The vertical lines beneath each actor show the actions and points of decision of the relevant actor. Additionally, the lines

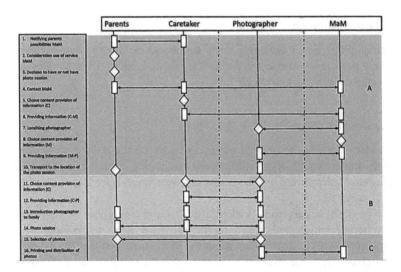

Figure 12.1 Praxeogram Process of Photoshoots

Legend:

Action	Border between spheres	(C) = caretaker
Interaction	Timeline Actor	M = MaM
Point of decision	Segment A, B, C	P = Photographer

Figure 12.1 Continued

between the actors show who is involved in which step of the process. Together, these actors, actions and decisions show how the common aim of the process (the photo session) is realized. This makes it possible to show in which parts of the process better alignment or improvement of the process is needed.

Role of the Researcher

Considering the emotional and difficult topic of this research and following the strict privacy rules that have been effective since 2018, complete anonymity of the participants was guaranteed. Findings that arose from this project can only be shared with other parties in consent with MaM, parents and supervisors. Prior to the interviews, each participant was asked permission to make audio recordings of the interview. These recordings were treated confidentially. Only both supervisors of this project have had the opportunity to read the transcripts of the interviews. Because of the sensitive topic of this research, bereavement and mourning, it was also crucially important for the researcher to be aware of her role during the research process. She tried to approach the bereaved parents with an open mind and empathy. The research group addressed the parents via e-mail with the request for participation, giving them time to think about their decision. After the parents' consent was obtained, the interview was held at a time and place that was convenient for the parents.

Interviews took place in 2016 (by Linssen) and in February and March 2017 (by Aans). The interviews were conducted in Dutch. For the purpose of this book, elements and quotes from the interviews have been translated to English. After the interviews, the parents were asked to reflect on the content of the interview and the role of the researcher and were given the opportunity to ask the researcher some questions. At times, it was challenging for her to keep the interviews on topic, and not let the conversation stray from the research topic, while still giving the parents the opportunity to tell their stories. The interviewer should be open and offer a listening ear, without crossing the border to a more therapeutic role (Beck & Konnert, 2007). The topic of the research is very sensitive and emotional for the parents, who had to relive the moment when they lost their child, and for the photographers, who had to talk about the heartrending situations they encountered during their work. In order to avoid negative psychological effects of the touching pictures and stories, Aans had several telephone sessions with a professional therapist.

In addition to the emotional aspects that were of influence, the researcher had to be aware of her own cultural lens. The (cultural) perspective of the researcher can possibly bias the research. In order to avoid this, the researcher used *decentring*: giving equal weight to the (cultural) perspectives of all people involved and letting go of one's own perspective (Spencer-Oatey & Franklin, 2009). By using triangulation of the research population, the researcher was able to take the perspectives of different groups into account. Avoiding subjectivity in such research is nearly impossible. However, by staying aware of her own cultural lens, she tried to avoid bias.

Another possible limitation is the time available for the project (10 weeks). It appeared difficult to reach and interview people of multiple cultural backgrounds in so short a period. This may have had a negative influence on the research, since it became difficult to consider the perspectives of different groups. The research was then limited to Dutch and atheist ($n = 5$), Turkish-Dutch and Muslim ($n = 3$) and Surinamese-Dutch and Hindu ($n = 1$) parents and caretakers, and Dutch photographers ($n = 10$).

Analysis

The process of arranging a photo session by Make a Memory was analysed and is displayed in the praxeogram (Figure 12.1). Presenting data in this way offered the people involved (photographer, MaM, hospital staff) the possibility to gain a clear insight in the structure and steps in a photo session. This, in turn, made it possible to assess the possibilities and challenges that arise during a photo session. It created understanding of the delicate and sensitive moments within the process, showing where there is room for improvement and better alignment.

The photographers indicated that most of the sessions take place in hospital. Therefore, it was decided to analyse the process of hospital photo sessions. The phases of the process were subdivided in segments (A, B and C). Segment A shows the phases that occur prior to the photo session. Segment B shows the time in hospital. In this segment, the photographer, the parents and the caretaker play crucial roles in the process. The final segment, C, involves the aftercare of the photo sessions. The most important actors in this segment are the photographer and MaM. The data show that segment B (hospital) contains the most crucial points of decision and interaction. Cultural assumptions and differences may have great impact on the process of the photo session. Phase 13 (introduction), for instance, included a crucial point of decision for one photographer when s/he believed the parents to be Muslim. S/he had to decide whether to shake hands with the bereaved mother and father, or not:

> There was a public discussion about this back then, about men, I believe football players, who refused to shake a female journalist's hand, because their religion does not allow that. And that was surely a woman, an African-looking woman, covered in veils, and a man with a beard. And then I entered, and I thought . . . should I . . . and they kept looking at me strangely, and then I thought: should I shake her hand or not? That moment felt really uncomfortable, and I did not shake her hand in the end . . . but maybe that was terribly impolite of me.
>
> (Participant 9, photographer, translation from Dutch)

A second phenomenon that is of impact on the process is the number of people present in the room of the photo session. The interviews with the photographers showed that there are significant differences between cultural groups in the number of people present in the room:

> And ehm the room was packed with people, I think there were over 15 people there. All with their cellphones taking pictures, and that child was handed from one to the other. And the nurse and I, we were standing there, and I thought: I cannot take pictures of this scene, I cannot even reach the child. That child was crying the whole time.
>
> (Participant 8, photographer, translated from Dutch)

A third observation of the process made it clear that (the perceiving of) power distance is an occurring cultural phenomenon that influences the process. The photographers stated during the interviews that they experience high power distance as uncomfortable when they feel the position of the woman in the relationship of the parents is different from what they are used to. Several other (cultural) phenomena affecting the photoshoots also emerged from the interviews, for example the presence of a religious caretaker, Islamic or Christian rituals, a distant attitude towards the child, the emotional state of the parents, the way parents evaluate the photo session and the pictures (composition, needs and wishes).

It appears that situational factors (one-off, short contact, little interaction) gave rise to an essentialist approach of the photographers to the parents (Dervin, 2015). Based on name, rituals and physical appearance, the photographers ascribed religious/cultural characteristics to the parents. Several phenomena detected in this research may seem strange from a western perspective.

Consultancy and Acceptance

The research (Aans, 2017) has shown that the families that request photoshoots reflect the notion of superdiversity (Vertovec, 2007). Superdiversity refers to individual client relations in which social workers (or in this case photographers) must be able to work with clients (here, parents) of diverse backgrounds (Hoffman, Geldof, & Koning, 2014). The variety of cultural backgrounds that the Dutch photographers encounter in their work is wide. In addition, within these cultural groups there is considerable variation. It is important that the photographers acknowledge these intracultural differences, and learn how to deal with, and anticipate on, the different needs of the parents. The praxeogram displays the different lines of action and points of decision. It appears that communication between the people involved (MaM, photographer, hospital staff) should be improved. Different segments within the praxeogram show that photographers should be provided with more information before arriving at the hospital.

A second result to emerge from this research is that taking pictures of (deceased) children might still be a taboo in some cultures. It appeared that photographers might find it difficult to cope with, and show understanding for, families that are not so willing to have these pictures taken of their child. The interviews have shown that rituals whereby an imam is present during a photoshoot can be counterproductive for the photographer. Misunderstandings about accompanying rituals can lead to a feeling of uncertainty with the photographers and the parents.

The different views on mourning also cause misunderstandings between photographer and client. It emerged that the photographers' views on the way in which people should mourn a deceased child at times differ from those of people from different cultural backgrounds. An example is the willingness, or lack thereof, to accept a photoshoot by MaM; taking pictures of deceased children may not be an appropriate form of mourning for all involved.

Another aspect that is affected by cultural misunderstandings is some parents being less inclined to reject a photographer's suggestions during a photoshoot. It appeared that the Dutch parents in this research were very likely to come up with their own suggestions (e.g. in composition), and to reject those of the photographers. Parents from other cultural backgrounds indicated during the interviews that they were less inclined to do so. This could lead to parents receiving pictures that they did not appreciate as much as was hoped. A possible explanation for this phenomenon may be found in Goffman's face theory.

The main goal of this research was to indicate where the problems occur in the process of a MaM photo session that the photographers experience, what causes misunderstandings and to give the photographers insights in ways to overcome misunderstandings and create mutual understanding. To reach this goal, the researcher provided a consultancy report with practical tips and advice. The tips are listed here, with the first three being general recommendations for MaM, and the final four recommendations for the photographers:

1. Create a practical infographic on the most frequently encountered cultural and religious rituals and conventions. This way, photographers are able to recognize and understand practices that they are unfamiliar with.
2. Strive for an even better cooperation between all participants involved (MaM, parents, medical specialists and photographers). The praxeogram showed that there are several points of decision in the process that need improvement in order to smoothen the process. In segment A, the receptionist of MaM should elicit more information from the person asking for the photoshoot, regarding for example the number of people present in the room and the need for religious caretakers to perform certain rituals.
3. Train intercultural interaction competences. Intercultural awareness provides the photographers with the ability to recognize different roles and obligations in interaction, and creates awareness of different politeness strategies. By means of intercultural trainings photographers can be given the opportunity to learn these competences.
4. Apply a dynamic and dialogic approach when in contact with bereaved parents. It is advisable to be open and apply a dynamic and dialogic approach. Photographers should focus on individual wishes and habits, instead of focusing on cultural backgrounds. Asking questions in a dialogue may keep them from explaining behaviour from their own perspective.
5. Reflect upon misunderstandings. After having experienced misunderstanding, reflect on the following questions: What was my contribution to the misunderstanding? What is the contribution of the other? What is the influence of ruling views, values, norms, meanings and opinions on the interaction? By means of reflection, lessons from the past may be learned and new misunderstandings avoided.
6. Do not just look at the differences but look for similarities. By shifting the focus from differences to similarities, photographers and parents can approach each other as equals. The focus then shifts from culture to individual (Hoffman et al., 2014).
7. Accept uncertainty and unpredictability. Every situation is different, and even though a good preparation can be helpful, the encounters between

photographer, children and parents will always be unpredictable. Awareness and acceptance of insecurities, not-knowing what is to come, and
of the clumsiness in interaction are necessary in order to cope with
diversity.

Final Reflection

After the research was completed, the researcher presented a summary of
the results and the advice to the board of the organization. The advice was
well received and put to practice. A folder with a summary of the most frequently occurring rituals and conventions was created. In addition, during
the annual meet-up for photographers and others involved with MaM, the
researcher offered a workshop regarding intercultural communication in the
context of the work of MaM. Prior to this workshop the photographers were
able to hand in descriptions of personal situations where they experienced
discomfort or misunderstanding during their work for MaM. The researcher
discussed these situations during the workshop, relating them to theories in
intercultural communication. This led to a lively discussion about actual situations, resulting in solutions for the photographers on how to handle these
encounters, and overcome uncertainties. Problems that were discussed during
the session resembled the problems and differences described in the research
report, such as dealing with differences in grief. Focal points of the workshop
were the following: developing awareness of one's own culture, the effect of
culture on communication, and behavioural flexibility in intercultural communication. Lastly, attendants of the workshop were encouraged to look for
similarities instead of differences in intercultural interactions. Afterwards,
the researcher received positive feedback from the organization as well as
from the photographers.

Note

1 Some of the data for this case study were collected by Michelle Linssen.

References

Aans, M (2017). Make a Memory: Een onderzoek naar de verschillende culturele
    rituelen en conventies bij gezinnen in rouw na het verlies van een kind (Master's
    thesis). Retrieved from https://studenttheses.library.uu.nl/search.php?language=en
Beck, A. M., & Konnert, C. A. (2007). Ethical issues in the study of bereavement: The
    opinions of bereaved adults. *Death Studies, 31*(9), 783–799.

Dervin, F. (2015). How to work with research participants: The researcher's role. In Z. Hua (Ed.), *Research methods in intercultural communication: A practical guide* (1st ed., pp. 135–146). Chichester, West Sussex and Malden, MA: Wiley Blackwell.

DeVault, M. L., & McCoy, L. (2001). Institutional ethnography: Using interviews to investigate relations. In J. F. Gubrium & J. A. Holstein (Eds.), *Handbook of interview research* (pp. 751–776). Thousand Oaks: Sage.

Ehlich, K., & Rehbein, J. (1972). Institutional ethnography. In A. Redder, J. Pauli, K. Bührig, & A. Redder (Eds.), *Praxeogrammem und Handlungsmuster als Methoden der Mehrsprachigkeitsanalyse: Mehrsprachige Kommunikation in der Stadt* (pp. 81–102). Das Beispiel Hamburg. Münster: Waxmann Verlag.

Goffman, E. (1967). On face-work. In *Interaction ritual* (pp. 5–45). New York, NY: Doubleday.

Hoffman, E., Geldof, D., & Koning, M. (2014). Superdiversiteit op de frontlijn: Diversiteitsbewuste communicatie is een noodzaak. *Alert: Tijdschrift voor Sociaal Werk en Politiek, 40*(4), 6–13.

Make a Memory. (2018). Retrieved from www.makeamemory.nl/

Spencer-Oatey, H., & Franklin, P. (2009). *Intercultural interaction: A multidisciplinary approach to communication.* Hampshire: Palgrave Macmillan.

Vertovec, S. (2007). Super-diversity and its implications. *Ethnic and Racial Studies, 30*(6), 1024–1054.

Concluding Chapter

*Roos Beerkens and Emmanuelle
Le Pichon-Vorstman*

Discussing these case studies with the authors and with graduate students in Intercultural Communication, we have reached a number of useful insights which will be presented in this concluding chapter. These concern the process of advisory projects and the importance of the contexts, and the way policymakers, commercial organizations, educators and non-profit organizations compare in this regard.

Advisers Can Hold Different Positions at Different Organizations

This book outlines steps in *research-based* advisory projects, applying knowledge and analytical skills to address questions of stakeholders. In fact, whereas all advisers in this book have a university degree, only two of the authors of the studies formally worked as consultants (case study 5 and 6). Some were employed by universities (study 1, 4 or 9), others worked for a foundation (study 11) or were graduate students on internships in organizations (study 2, 3, 10 and 12). This is why this book differs from what the reader may have read before: we adopted a research-based perspective from an interdisciplinary point of view. This was also reflected by the internal diversity of our teams. For example, in case study 6, the authors were at the time, a graduate intern, a university lecturer and a consultant from a consultancy firm, while the authors of case study 12 were a graduate student and a policy adviser. In other words, intercultural consultants are a diverse group, as diverse as the organizations they counsel, and we believe that this diversity allows the field to always move forward.

Advisers' Roles Differ and Show Fluidity

Not only the formal positions of the advisers show great variety, also the roles they take on in the consultancy process differ. The different roles exemplified in the studies are contingent on contextual factors, and on the choices the adviser makes. There is not one single, fixed role for advisers. Although Block (2011) stresses the importance of consensus about the role of the adviser at the beginning of the advisory process, our studies show that it may be extremely difficult to adhere to one role and that doing so might even interfere with the advisory process. In case study 11, Kambel and de Jong start off as experts, but as the project develops, their role switches to collaborative and later even to an "extra pair-of-hands" (see Block, 2011, pp. 15–16). In study 9, Lory takes a clear prescriptive approach in her advice and implementation. One of her research questions even entails the phrase, "how can . . . be convinced of". This is not something she decided by herself; it took negotiation skills and a collaborative approach to reach consensus on the goals. In study 4, which is comparable to study 9, ten Thije developed a prescriptive advice in cooperation with his client at the European Commission. He based this advice on academic research and his expertise in the field, resulting in an expert role. During the process, he was confronted with changes and contradictions within language policy of the European Commission and had to deal with representatives with different interests. Developing insight in the structural contradictions within international organizations is prerequisite for the adviser. In this case, it meant waiting for the client to come back after three years with a clear-cut question. This case also stresses the relevance of maintaining a long-standing relationship with a client instead of delivering instant advice. Our studies thus show that advisers' roles exhibit considerable variety and fluidity, demanding a flexible approach by making use of all the institutional and contextual knowledge that is gained during the process.

No Two Consultancy Processes Are the Same Although Similar Steps Are Taken

Talking to the advisers and discussing the cases, we learned that there is no such thing as a standard advisory process. All studies have different time spans and sequences of steps. However, we do recognize a certain pattern in the steps that need to be paid attention to, including for instance building a relationship with the client and identifying and contacting the stakeholders to debrief the problem in order to define the research steps. The approach needs to be agreed upon with the client, responsibilities distributed, data gathered, the results discussed and the advice written or presented or both. In some cases, advisers were asked to implement the advice. Therefore it is always essential to keep the client posted on the progress that is made throughout the consultancy process. However, advisers should always be aware that their interpretation of events may not be shared by the client or other stakeholders.

In fact, most intercultural communication experts are trained to be able to look at the case from different frames of reference and it seems essential to keep developing this crucial intercultural competence.

Additionally, the ability to build a harmonious relationship with clients is also a precondition for understanding their questions (see Spencer-Oatey & Franklin, 2009; Cole, 2019). Advisers are also people who are able to create trust, share responsibilities, acknowledge feelings (of resistance, frustration) and accept their own limitations (cf. Block, 2011). Advising others in order to improve intercultural understanding starts with our awareness of – and reflection on – our own biases and limitations.

Strengths of Applying Academic Expertise in Real-Life Contexts

Based on these twelve case studies, and in line with our situated approach, it becomes clear that, in situations of intercultural communication, attributing problems to mainly cultural differences, which Koole and ten Thije (1994, pp. 51–52) term "maximum interpretation", is a dangerous trap. In studies 2 and 6, the task of the researchers was to redirect the focus from differences in cultural backgrounds to other contributors to possible communication break-downs. In study 9, the ideologies of school stakeholders on languages and cultures needed to be addressed in order to foster the implementation of new plurilingual pedagogies. Lory thus transformed the perception of an inter-cultural problem into an intercultural opportunity. In study 1, the researchers were asked to support a client with a problem that seemed to threaten the cli-ent's daily work. They, too, translated a problem into an opportunity. Advice was based on the advisers' intercultural competence, which enabled them to shift frames of reference.

Beyond a European Perspective

Although the studies described in this book were conducted in different parts of the world, in the Netherlands, Canada, the Antilles, Suriname, Belgium and Saudi Arabia, all advisers had a European background. As our perspec-tive is situated, we do not aim to dispense universal knowledge. In fact, our goal was to show that in each study, several cultural levels play a role at the same time, and that by being able to disentangle and interpret them, each adviser may bring valuable insights to the clients. Differences between orga-nizational cultures based on their structures played an important role in study 5, while study 11 insisted on the history of human rights and its impact on culture. Gaining knowledge about possible levels of culture, like the advisers of these studies did, is essential, as is being aware of our own cultural and normative biases.

This book introduced a new perspective to those working in the fields of consultancy and intercultural communication, the core message being that a situated mutual understanding and a more pluralistic orientation have become essential elements in the process of advising.

Further Reading and References

Block, P. (2011). *Flawless consulting: A guide to getting your expertise used.* San Francisco, CA: Pfeiffer.

Cole, D. (2019). Looking for rapport in the metacommunicative features of an ethnographic interview. In Z. Goebek (Ed.), *Understanding rapport.* Berlin: Mouton De Gruyter.

Koole, T., & ten Thije, J. D. (1994). *The construction of intercultural discourse: Team discussions of educational advisers.* Utrecht studies in language and communication (Vol. 2). Amsterdam: Rodopi.

Spencer-Oatey, H., & Franklin, P. (2009). *Intercultural interaction: A multidisciplinary approach to intercultural communication.* Hampshire: Palgrave Macmillan.

Subject Index

academic consultant 9
adviser 134
advisory process 2, 135
agency 3, 9
anonymity of the participants 127
Aruba 34
asylum seekers 105, 110
atheist 128
awareness training 48, 50

Belbin team-role assessment 67, 69
Belgium 83
bereaved parents 124, 131
bias 10, 128, 136
bilingual education 77
British 66

Canada 93, 96
caretaker 126, 128
children 16, 20, 77, 85, 124
client 2, 8, 20, 57, 66, 78, 125, 130, 135
code switching 79
cognates 97
Collaborative Social Design-based
    research 95
colonization 114
communication xx, 2, 6, 23, 36, 46, 58,
    62, 69, 109, 117
communication audit 37
communication network 60, 106
communication plan 58, 62
communication platform 34, 110
communication style 70
communicative means 5, 62
community language 77

community of practice 98
community researcher 116, 121
consultancy 2, 8, 88
consultancy process 9, 20, 134
consultant 2, 8
consultation 2, 8
content-based language teaching 84, 89
cross-border mergers 57
cultural and linguistic understanding 122
cultural background 1, 5, 8, 28, 78, 122,
    128, 130
cultural conventions 125
cultural diversity 22, 69, 93, 99
cultural lens 128
cultural match 116
culture 6, 8, 23, 69

deaf and hard of hearing 105, 110
deaf culture 107
death and mourning 125
digitalization 5
diversity 10, 23, 35, 69, 132, 134
double loyalty 31
Dutch (culture/society) 15, 30, 107, 121,
    124, 130
Dutch (language) 34, 36, 40, 45, 83,
    113, 128
Dutch sign language 109
dynamic view on culture 7

Egyptian 66
emic 23
employment agencies 29
English 34, 36, 40, 43, 49, 51, 70, 94
English as lingua franca 50

essentialist approach 2, 129
essentialist view on culture 6, 8, 10
ethics committee 20
ethnocentric 10, 70, 73
ethnocentrism 8
ethnographic approach 95, 126
ethnographic fieldwork/studies 23
ethnographic observation 59
ethnographic perspective 8
ethnorelative perspective 73
European Commission 45, 52
expatriates 78
experiential learning exercises 72
external communication 36

face theory 130
fieldwork 23
Flanders 83
Flemish 83
flexibility 63
French xviii, 45, 93

German 45
globalization xviii, 1
governance 116
government 116
grammar 79

Hindu 128
Hogan Personality Inventory 70
holistic process 99
home languages 83, 90

identity 6, 8, 41, 79, 81
imam 126, 130
immigrant 24, 29
implementation 58, 64, 85, 88, 96,
    121, 135
inclusion 15
inclusive 70, 94, 97, 99
in-depth interviews 19, 126
indigenous nations 116
indigenous peoples/communities 113
infographic 131
informed consent 39, 120
integration process 57
interactionist view on culture 7
intercomprehension 45
intercultural adviser 10

intercultural awareness 71, 131
intercultural communication 5, 8, 20, 23
intercultural competence 9, 81, 136
intercultural consultancy 1, 8
intercultural consultant 9, 134
intercultural interaction competences
    125, 131
interculturality 120
intercultural mediation 31
intercultural opportunity 3, 136
intercultural understanding 1, 136
interdisciplinary 20, 134
internal communication 36, 40
internationalization 1, 5
interpreter 106, 109
intervention 1, 19, 60, 71, 86, 95
interview 19, 23, 36, 47, 50, 59, 67, 87,
    108, 117, 126
Islamic or Christian rituals 129
Italian 45
iterative 58, 126

Kari'na 113
Kindergarten teachers 84, 85, 90

labour migrants 22, 30
land management plan 115, 118
language acquisition 78, 83
language awareness movement 93
language development 79, 86, 97
language policy 19, 45, 49, 83, 135
language proficiency 79, 85
language(s) of instruction 36, 83, 94
language test 87
language use 47, 79
leadership 58, 66, 117
leadership style 69
Likert-scale 66
Limburg 22, 84
lingua franca 46, 48
lingua receptiva 46
linguistic background 48
linguistic closeness 49
linguistic competence 48, 79, 81
linguistic diversity 22, 93, 99
linguistic insecurity 96
linguistic landscape 25, 96
literature review 36, 80, 96
local community/communities 23, 30

local governments 23, 29
Lokono 113
Lower-Marowijne Area 113
luistertaal 46

management 19, 37, 40, 57, 70,
    107, 115
maximum interpretation 136
mediator xx, 78, 98
medical experts 126
migrants 15, 22, 28, 78
minority language 77, 94, 97
miscommunication 43
misunderstanding 57, 130
mixed marriages 78
Model Village Constitution 118
monoglossic 94
monolingual curriculum 97
monolingual paradigm 93, 98
Moroccan 66
multiculturality 1
multilingual communication 43
multilingual competencies 50
multilingualism 23, 45, 52, 83
multilingual mode 48, 50
municipality 15, 23, 29
Muslim 128
mutual intelligibility 46, 51, 79
mutual trust 20, 72, 122
mutual understanding 24, 78, 107,
    131, 137

national culture 70
The Netherlands 15, 22, 57, 78, 105
newly arrived migrant pupils 15

observation 23, 36, 65, 87
organizational cultures 57, 59, 63,
    69, 136

Papiamento 34, 40
parents 77, 124, 126
participant observation 23, 36
pedagogical counsellors 95, 98
pedagogical practices 94, 99
photographer 124, 130
pluri-identities 94
plurilingual paradigm 94, 98
plurilingual pedagogical practice 93
plurilingual pedagogies 136

plurilingualism 94, 98
police 24, 28
policy 16, 20, 45, 52, 78, 84, 96, 99
policy adviser 134
policymakers 16, 79
Polish 22, 29
politeness 131
Portuguese 49
power distance 70, 129
powerful learning environment 84
praxeogram 126, 130
priest 126
primary school 15, 83
proficiency-based language teaching 84
pupils 15, 93

qualitative method(s) 18, 87, 108, 126
quantitative method(s) 7, 18, 87
questionnaire 19, 37, 47, 67, 85, 117

receptive competencies 45
receptive multilingualism 45
recommendations 19, 29, 48, 71, 81,
    111, 131
recordings 23, 127
reflection 8, 50, 72, 94, 98, 131, 136
refugees 105
religious 7, 73, 124, 129
research-based 9, 77, 134
rituals (and conventions) 124, 131

Saudi Arabia 66, 70, 73
school achievements 17
school-internal coaches 84, 89
second language acquisition 78
second language understanding 18
self-awareness 71
self-determination 119, 122
self-image 67
self-reflection 71
self-rule 116
semi-structured interviews 19, 38, 50,
    67, 108, 117, 126
social representations 95, 98
societal view on culture 7
Spanish 34, 49
Sranan 113, 122
stakeholders 17, 20, 30, 60, 66, 88, 107,
    111, 135
statistics 60, 69

stereotypes 8, 73
strategic orientation 116
superdiversity 130
Suriname 113
Surinamese Dutch 122, 128
survey 24, 66, 81, 87
sustainability (of language) 94
SWOT 115

task-based language education/teaching 84, 86
teacher 18, 84, 88, 93
team retreat 71
team survey 72

therapeutic role 128
topic list 38, 108
transcript 39, 126
translation 45
transnational mobility 93
triangulation 37, 126, 128
Turkish-Dutch 128

uncertainty 130, 131
unpredictability 131

village constitution 118

Yemeni 66

Name Index

Aans, M. 130
Abdallah-Pretceille, M. 7
Adler, P. 6
Adrian, A. 37
Agar, M. xx
Allard, R. 96
Amas, N. 109
Anderson, T. 95
Appel, R. 79
Armand, F. 93, 94, 97

Baarda, B. 38, 39
Baauw, S. 19
Backus, A. 45, 51
Balcaite, I. 16, 17
Bamberger, F. 34
Bangou, F. 94, 95, 97
Barmeyer, C. 57, 60
Batavier, K. 106, 108
Beatson, A. 37
Beck, A. M. 128
Beerkens, R. 46
Belbin, R. M. 67, 69
Belfi, B. 83
Bennett, M. J. 73
Berben, M. 88
Berghuis, A. 113
Blain, S. 94
Block, P. 9, 135, 136
Blom, L. 78, 81
Blommaert, J. 22, 95
Boeije, H. 24
Bolhuis, J. C. 70
Boruta, D. 23, 24, 25, 28, 30, 31

Buytendijk, E. 106, 108
Byers-Heinlein, K. 80

Cammarata, L. 94
Canagarajah, S. 3, 9
Candelier, M. 93
Cantone, K. F. 80
Carroll, K. S. 36
Cavanagh, M. 94
Ceginskas, V. 6
Colchester, M. 120
Cole, D. 136
Collins, J. 95
Cornelis, L. 9
Cornell, S. 116
Cornips, L. 22, 23
Cortois, L. 83
Cummins, J. 93

Dagenais, D. 93
De Goede, M. 38, 39
De Jong, C. 113
Demont, P. xvii
De Roo, B. 89
De Rooij, V. 22, 23
Dervin, F. 7, 129
De Swart, H. 6
Dettwyler, K. A. 7, 8
DeVault, M. L. 126
Deveau, K. 96
De Vries, J. 47, 48, 50, 52
D'Iribarne, P. 7
Dörnyei, Z. 37, 38
Doukakis, I. 37

Downs, C. 37
Dumcius, R. 16, 17

Edelmann, D. 10
Ehlich, K. 126
Evaristo, J. R. 7

Fan, W. 17
Farhan Ferrari, M. 120
Farmer, D. 97
Fleuret, C. 94, 95, 97
Flores, N. 9
Franklin, P. 7, 9, 28, 125, 128, 136

Geldof, D. 130, 131
Geoffroy, C. xvii
Gérin-Lajoie, D. 94, 95
Goffman, E. 125
Gogolin, I. 93
Gorter, D. 45, 51
Gumperz, J. J. xx

Hoffman, E. 130, 131
Hofstede, G. 6, 70
Hofstede, G. J. 70
Hogan, J. 70
Hogan, R. 70
Hogendoorn, M. 37
Holliday, A. 6
Huttova, J. 16, 17
Hyde, M. 6

Ibrahim, A. 94, 95, 97

Jodelet, D. 98
Johnston, K. 37
Jorgensen, M. 116
Juffermans, K. 22

Kalt, J. 116
Kambel, E.-R. 113, 114
Karahanna, E. 7
Karanges, E. 37
Kayser, W. 71
Kim, Y. Y. 7
Kirkpatrick, J. 71
Knapp, K. 45, 51
Kok, G. 9

Koning, M. 130, 131
Konnert, C. A. 128
Koole, T. 136
Kotter, J. P. 88
Kroon, S. 22
Kullman, J. 6

Lagnado, J. 109
Lamoureux, S. 97
Landry, R. 96
Lanza, E. 80
Lasagabaster, D. 96
Le Pichon-Vorstman, E. 6, 19, 113
Leurebourg, R. 94, 97
Leuverink, K. 34
Lings, I. 37
Loman, F. 89
Lory, M.-P. 94, 97
Luo, L. 109

MacKay, F. 114
MacSwan, J. 80
Mayrhofer, U. 57, 60
Maznevski, M. L. 73
McCoy, L. 126
Meisel, I. M. 80
Minkov, M. 70
Moons, C. 83, 89
Muysken, P. 79

Nicaise, I. 16, 17
Nicollin, L. 93

OECD 83
Ogay, T. 10
Ooijevaar, J. 23

Porila, A. 23
Postma, H. 50
Prasad, G. 95
Proctor, T. 37

Rampton, B. 7, 8
Rehbein, J. 23, 46, 126
Rogerson-Revell, P. 70
Rosa, J. 93
Rousseau, C. 97
Ruck, B. 9, 17

Salario, T. 70
Schein, E. 65
Schjerve-Rindler, R. 45, 51
Schuytn, V. 89
Serratrice, L. 77
Shattuck, J. 95
Siarova, H. 16, 17
Slembrouck, S. 95
Sluiter, N. 23
Spencer-Oatey, H. 7, 9, 28, 125,
   128, 136
Spilde, K. 116
Spotti, M. 22
Sriramesh, K. 37
Srite, M. 7
Statistique Canada. 93
Stengs, I. 22, 23
Strobbe, L. 83
Svalberg, A. 93
Swanenberg, J. 45, 51

Ten Thije, J. D. 7, 23, 45, 46, 48, 51, 136

Van Avermaet, P. 83
Van Damme, J. 83
Van den Bergh, H. 6
Van den Branden, K. 83, 84, 88
Van der Hulst, M. 38, 39

Van der Knaap, D. 7
Van Der Wildt, A. 83
Van Gorp, K. 83, 84, 89
Van Houtte, M. 83
Van Klaveren, S. 47, 48, 50
Van Ravenstein, I. 9
Van Rooij, S. 106, 108
Verčič, A. 37
Verčič, D. 37
Verhelst, M. 83, 85, 89
Verschik, A. 46
Verschuren, S. 23
Versteden, P. 89
Vertovec, S. 130
Vetter, E. 45, 51
Vorstman, J. 19

Wang, X. 22
Ward, K. 109
Weick, K. E. 59
Weitzner, V. 120
Werker, J. F. 80
Wery, A. 50
Wijckmans, B. 89
Wildemuth, B. M. 109
Wołoszyn, P. 22, 23, 24, 29,
   30, 31
Wolters, C. A. 17